Astrology and Prediction

1 The signs of the Zodiac: from Leopold of Austria's *Astrorum Scientia*, 1489

Astrology and Prediction

Eric Russell

Drake Publishers Inc
New York

ISBN 87749-329-4

Published in 1973 by
Drake Publishers Inc
381 Park Avenue South
New York, N.Y. 10016

Printed in Great Britain

CONTENTS

THE ILLUSTRATIONS

ACKNOWLEDGEMENT

The Author and the Publisher wish to thank Aldus Books for permission to reproduce figs. 13, 21 and 29, the horoscope (cast by Jeff Mayo) on p. 128 and the illustrations of the houses, aspects, zodiacal signs and planets on pp. 130-48, which are taken from Louis MacNeice *Astrology*, and for lending a number of other illustrations that appeared in this book. Acknowledgement is also due to: American Federation of Astrologers for fig. 32; Bettman Archive, fig. 42; Bibliothèque Nationale, fig. 36; British Museum, figs. 3, 5, 7, 8, 11, 17, 20, 22-4, 35 and 37-9; Culver Pictures Inc., fig. 28; Mansell Collection, figs. 9, 10, 12 and 40-1; Musée du Louvre, fig. 6; Popperphoto, figs. 2 and 31; *Radio Times* Hulton Picture Library, figs. 18, 27 and 30; Staatliche Museum, Berlin, fig. 4; Uffizi Gallery, Florence, figs. 15-16; Victoria and Albert Museum, fig. 1.

Chapter 1
The Uncertain Frontier

Late on a November night in 1560, a podgy, middle-aged woman, dressed in heavy widow's weeds, laboriously climbed the steeply winding steps of an ancient tower in Salon, Provence. At the top, she entered a kind of ante-chamber and there sat waiting patiently – indeed, humbly – although she had power of life and death over the man she had come to see. In his own good time he admitted her into the inner room, a chamber that was part laboratory and part study, and began the ritual which was the reason for her presence. Tracing a magic circle upon the ground, he seated her within it and then drew up before her a table upon which lay a disc of polished steel. Inscribed in pigeon's blood around the disc were three Hebrew names of God – JEHOVA, MITTATRON, ADONAI. After an interval, the disc clouded over and a crowned male figure appeared in it and walked once around its perimeter. The figure was succeeded by three more crowned males, each of whom made a certain number of turns around the perimeter of the disc before disappearing. All four figures were successively kings of France : three of them were the sons of the myopically peering woman for she was Catherine de' Medici, Queen Regent of France and the elderly magician was the physician commonly known as Nostradamus.

It is a simple enough task to reconstruct the mechanics of what happened in the turret room on that autumn night for the 'science of mirrors' was a common enough technique and descriptions of it abound. What, if anything, actually appeared in the mirror was known only to the two people involved. It is unlikely that the highly discreet Nostradamus would have gossiped on a matter which could only too easily be termed treasonable. The overwhelming probability is that Catherine de' Medici recorded, or passed on, what she saw or thought she saw. There was nothing unusual about this. The dumpy little Italian woman, who ran a great kingdom like her forbears had run a city and who, in all other matters, considered only what was practical and best for her family, wholly and utterly believed in astrology and regulated matters accordingly. This woman who planned, quite placidly, the Massacre of St Bartholomew and lost not a night's sleep afterwards, was reduced to a state of gibbering terror when a comet appeared over France, because 'the crazy astrologers say that it presages the death of a queen or great lady in some terrible manner', as a contemporary noted. Yet she seems to have had grounds for her wholly irrational belief – not least in that matter of the divination by mirror. Her three sons did indeed succeed each other in her lifetime. But the fourth successor to the throne was their despised cousin whom everyone considered to be an also ran – and who came to the throne after her death.

Catherine de' Medici's subjects also saw nothing unusual about her obsession. Life – visible, physical life – was only an extension of a larger world. The belief had nothing to do with education, nothing to do with intellect. Martin Luther firmly believed in the goblins of his ancestors and was plagued by the Devil himself in a very real form; James I of England took time off from his monarchical duties to investigate the prevalence of demons. It was but a short step from the belief in a world running parallel to this, to the belief that events in the physical world were being continuously foreshadowed in the intangible world. The elegant complex structure of astrology could be adequately manipulated only by highly qualified professionals who demanded high fees for their craft. There were hedgerow astrologers, even as there were hedgerow physicians, who would foretell the future for a few coppers or even a piece of bread and a jug of ale. But most people sought their view into the future through traditional forms that had not varied for centuries – the chance patterns formed by natural objects, the fall of dice or cards or bones, the flight of birds, the wise woman mumbling over some favoured object that induced mild self-hypnosis. Men did not question the validity or significance: they existed as grammar and language existed. The only problem was to interpret what they transmitted.

The greatest puzzle to posterity are those universal signs which thousands believed to mark some important coming event—usually dire. They imply frequent and widespread mass hallucinations that have almost totally disappeared from society: the most dramatic modern example is the Angels of Mons which probably owe their fame more to subsequent newspaper articles than to the number of contemporary witnesses. But such experiences were once commonplace. In 1494, shortly before the traumatic French invasion of Italy, there were well documented reports of terrible portents – gigantic warriors battling in the sky, showers of blood, of stones; birth of monsters. The onset of plague invariably provided a crop of such portents: so too did bad harvests.

The twentieth century, pre-eminently the century of rationalism and scepticism, began by dismissing outright such claims to precognition. In June 1927 Count Harry Kessler, German socialite and politician, recorded in his copious diary the account of a conversation – or, rather, an argument – that he had listened to at dinner that evening. Two of his fellow guests were Gerhardt Hauptmann, the playwright, and Albert Einstein. Hauptmann asked Einstein what he thought of astrology, ' obviously anticipating that Einstein would allow it some significance or other. Einstein, however, rejected it utterly and in as gruff a manner as, given his conciliatory character, he is capable of. The Copernican system, he declared conclusively, made a clean sweep of the anthropocentric view of the entire firmament as revolving round the earth and humanity. Faith in the influence of demons is probably at the root of concepts of causality. (Clearly what he meant was that man's notions have evolved from faith in demons to faith in astrology, i.e. in the influence of the stars: and from there, via the Copernican system, to the causal doctrine of a purely mechanistic interpretation of nature.)

So, neatly and tidily, the greatest living scientist disposed of the old ragbag of odds and ends that was astrology and prediction. No man could accuse Albert Einstein of bigotry, of a narrowly materialist view of the universe and if a brain such as his could see nothing of astrological prediction but a hangover from a primitive belief in demons then there was little else to be said for it.

But at about the time that this little German Jew momentarily took his eyes off receding galaxies to glance scornfully at the nonsense of astrology, a Swiss, burrowing deep into the human psyche, encountered what seemed to be a series of inexplicable patterns, although it was not until 1950 that C. G. Jung gave formal shape to what he called 'synchronicity.' It was impossible to believe in 'astral influences,' to believe in any chain of events predictable by the movement of the planets: that belief was as remote as belief in the philosophers' stone. But there were patterns of events in which otherwise wholly irrelevant factors seems to be related—the clock which stopped upon its owner's death; the cycles of 'good' and 'bad' luck which characterised every human life; the sensation known under the clumsy name of déjà vu. Groping for a key to these phenomena, Jung noted that: 'The primitive mentality has always explained synchronicity as magical causality, right down to our own day and on the other hand, philosophy assumed a meaningful connection between natural events until well into the eighteenth century. I prefer the latter hypothesis.' It was, after all, only another way of stating the ancient belief that all things were related, that all things tended to unity. Jung took the belief a stage further into the realm of science by studying the horoscopes of 483 marriages, comparing them with a like number of unmarried persons. There did indeed seem to be some relationship between the state of being married, and the horoscopes of those who were married – certain planetary conjunctions which astrology always associated with the married condition appeared more frequently in the horoscopes of the married than the unmarried.

Jung considered his researches to be inconclusive and turned to more rewarding fields. But not so the professional or traditional astrologer – usually, but not always the same person. Astrology had taken a heavy beating over the matter of its total failure to predict the outbreak of World War II. Now it had been handed an excuse from a completely unimpeachable source. For a short period ' synchronicity' was all the fashion in that small segment of the astrological world whose members actually thought out the implications of their beliefs. For centuries and probably for millennia, astrologers had taught that if, say, the planet Mercury were in a certain position in the heavens, then certain things would happen on earth – in the case of Mercury's influence a period of restlessness, a time when quick-thinking, light-fingered men would have it all their own way. Now, however, citing the famous psychologist the astrologers could claim that Mercury did not *cause* this specific result: it merely synchronised with it in what Jung called ' a psychically conditioned relativity of space and time '.

But while astrologers were attempting to fit Jung's austere utterances into their baroque world, a young French graduate of the Sorbonne, Michel Gauquelin, provided them with the most impressive scientific credentials, even though he contemptuously dismissed their pretensions. Gauquelin was a statistician and his interest had been aroused by an experiment rather similar to Jung's. A French astrologer, Léen Lasson,

B

appeared to have established the relationship between certain planets and certain types of profession: in the traditional manner Mercury dominated in the horoscopes of writers, Venus in that of artists, Mars that of generals. The total number of horoscopes involved, however, were far too few to eliminate the possibility of chance and Gauquelin decided to take the matter a step further: he established a test list of 576 leading physicians and then looked for any dominant astrological characteristic linking them as a group. He found that Mars and Saturn appeared in the horoscopes in a manner which could not be dismissed as chance.

Gauquelin now vastly extended the field of enquiry by collecting the birth data of 5,000 eminent Frenchmen. They included members of all the leading professions – lawyers, doctors, artists, musicians, writers, soldiers. They appeared to have nothing in common save their eminence and their professions. Nevertheless, after months of work Gauquelin was able to group them almost wholly by the planet rising at their birth. Mars and Saturn did predominate in the horoscopes of scientists; Mercury predominated in that of writers, Jupiter in that of sportsmen. Gauquelin published the results of his research but his fellow statisticians were unimpressed. It was a fluke, they declared, a pattern which was applicable only to France. Gauquelin grimly set about creating a test condition which could not possibly be faulted, taking all Europe as his province with a total of 25,000 eminent people and again the pattern was established. All soldiers did not have Mars in the ascendant, nor did all writers have Mercury but in each group the incidence of the astrologically relevant planet was such as to take it out of the realm of chance.

Gauquelin's reaction to this ancient puzzle is highly characteristic of this century: when faced with an apparently inexplicable phenomenon – measure it. The act of measuring usually has to be its own reward: in this particular incident the statistician, while firmly rejecting any astrological or occult interpretation, was wholly unable to account for the pattern.

Over the past generation or so the number of sporadic raids into this twilight field has increased, but the results remain disappointingly thin, dissolving when subjected to really intense investigation. In the thirties J. W. Dunne's book, *An Experiment With Time,* seemed to mark the first real advance in the analysis of precognition. It begins with his account of a vision or dream in which he saw, not a future event, but a newspaper report of it, and thereafter builds up his complex theory of a serial universe of receding observers. But though Dunne's experience may very well have been real, his methods of selecting phenomena for analysis did not stand that test of close inspection and his book is now looked on more as an oddity than the beginning of a scientific analysis. Later, J. B. Rhine's work on ESP at Duke's University seemed a more solid, more widely based investigation. In the 1940s and 1950s no science fiction novel with any pretensions to verisimilitude could fail to make a ritual obeisance towards Rhine. Here, again, it seemed as though a map were being drawn up of a twilit area – a map in which there were many blank spots but where the main roads were clearly marked so that other investigators could follow and extend the frontiers of the known world. Telepathy, telekinesis, 'the sixth sense' generally, all these together with the precognitive faculties came at last under sober investigation after being, for so long, in the province of the occultist, the mystic, the crank and the charlatan. But again an examination of the evidence from a different angle produced different results, demolishing the brave structure raised on reason and deduction and observation. There was a very slight gain, a slight extension not of the frontier but of the road leading to it. It was now hardly possible to deny that some non-tangible, non-measurable faculty produced by a sense other than the recognised five actually existed. But what its significance was, or who was likely to possess it, or how it could be employed, or anything else about it remained as mysterious as when investigations first started.

The firm confidence that rational investigation would produce rational answers began to wane in the early fifties and in its place began a resurgence of the old, colourful semi-occult beliefs ranging from tarot cards to astrology via cheiromancy and cartomancy. The most dramatic evidence of that was in 1962 when Indian astrologers predicted the imminent end of the world, due to a most unusual conjunction of planets. The vast majority of the human race stolidly went about its affairs but here and there Noah-like groups took it seriously. In Britain, a Mr Tapsell led a body of fellow devotees to the summit of Coniston Old Man in the Lake District where an energetic prayer-session delivered the world – and Britain with it – from the most recent of a long series of eschatological dooms. Significantly, it was the ancient and once royal art of astrology that was responsible for the prediction and the small, but very real, reaction of panic. Although only one out of many predictive systems, in the second half of the twentieth century astrology was again emerging from a long period of obscurity and abasement as it had emerged so often in the past.

2 C. G. Jung, whose theory of synchronicity conferred a respectability on astrology

3 Head of a god in the form of intestines used for divination
Babylon seventh century BC

Chapter 2
The History of the Future

Astrology came into being in Babylon. Its precise place of birth was a chamber, a temple-tower on the flat crown of an artificial hill called a ziggurat. There were many of these ziggurats dotted around the city and its environs, built by men with faint, nostalgic memories of mountains who found themselves established in the centre of a vast, flat plain. The tower on the ziggurat served as a temple-cum-observatory and laboratory for there is, as yet, no distinction between art and religion and science. Within the temple the priest-scientists – plump, dark-skinned men with impassive faces – not only discharge the rites of religion but patiently, brilliantly work, into one great synthesis, elements from half a dozen cultures. Aesthetically, the completed synthesis will be pleasing because the workers have a very high degree of sensitivity. The practical aspect of the work, however, is probably more important for what these men are trying to do is to create a map of the future. They believe that, given time and the accumulation of knowledge – and the goodwill of the god – it is just as possible to create such a map as it is to lay out the plan of a city, or write the history of the past.

The search for such a map had begun, consciously or unconsciously, at that moment when some brain – perhaps only part human – pondered on the relationship between seed and flower, between lightning and fire, between departure and arrival. It did not even require a human brain to employ prediction as part of the business of living, using it as regularly and in as matter of fact a way as breathing. The tiger predicts that a spring of a given energy will take it on to the back of a fleeing victim and, before it even moves into action, further predicts that the victim will, in fact, be edible or vulnerable. The faculty operates at the elemental, totally non-conscious level, for even the seed is predicting that sunlight lies above the dark earth and so grows towards it. The human, or semi-human desire to make some provision for the future serves to raise the faculty from the purely instinctive stage to the beginnings of an art and of a religion. The variegation of the seasons was, perhaps, the first and certainly the most obvious of long-term, but recurrent variations. Admittedly some animals recognised the same variations and made their own provisions – squirrels storing nuts in the autumn against the hunger of winter, bears adapting themselves to the same problem by turning their own bodies into larders, swallows flying south. But the hairy, grunting, shambling animal that might, perhaps, not yet be man added a new dimension, turning to a force outside himself to guide, forewarn and preserve.

In the beginning, in the day of the hunters, it was a straightforward enough proposition for the man with the greatest cunning and the strongest weapon was the man best equipped to deal with ferocious or fleetfooted game. The quarry could, perhaps, be trapped in a magical net, its future fate painted up in bright colours, creating in the now what would happen in the then so that its ferocity would be sapped, its fleetness hampered by the knowledge of impending doom. The death of the beast was the death of a brother – for who could tell animal from human blood? – so therefore the same rites that propitiated the human dead and kept their envious ghosts at bay would serve to propitiate the humbler brother.

But when at last the farmer came uncertainly, timidly, on

the stage, gathering up his unimpressive husks and fruits and seeds, he needed something quite different from this blood magic, something at once more practical and more subtle. The vulnerable seed, laid in the unyielding earth, must have seemed infinitely vulnerable, infinitely precious. How best, therefore, to give it a reasonable chance against the demons of heat and cold and drought? And when it had lain its term in the ground and, miraculously, brought forth its increase, when should that increase be harvested? From these two similar needs arose two contrasting systems – the purely practical mystique of the meteorologist and the sympathetic magic of the poet or the priest.

There was, at first, almost certainly no distinction between the practical and the metaphysical, because the prophet who foretold the ideal weather when the crop should be harvested was employing the same technique as the poet or philosopher who declaimed when the crop should be planted. The mysterious emanations from the pinpoints of light in the night sky controlled the growing plant, even as they controlled the wind and the rain and the thunder.

What makes the cornfields happy, under what constellation. It's best to turn the soil, my friend, and train the vine On the elm . . .

So Virgil opens *The Georgics,* prefacing a basically practical work, with the flat statement that the position of the stars at a particular time will govern certain vital tasks in farming.

BABYLON AND ASSYRIA

When Jupiter stands in front of Mars there will be corn and men will be slain, or a great army will be slain.
When Mars approaches Jupiter there will be great devastation in the land.
When the moon rideth in a chariot, the yoke of the king of Akkad will prosper.

When the moon is low in appearance the submission of a far country will come to the king.

When Mercury culminates in Tammuz, there will be corpses. When Leo is dark, the heart of the land will not be happy.

When Jupiter goes with Venus, the prayers of the land will reach the heart of the gods.

This collection of precepts or reports, drawn up for Assurbanipal, the king of Assyria, form the oldest surviving collection of astrological predictions. They appeared at a comparatively late period of Mesopotamian civilisation for originally the interpretative skills of the priests were devoted to dreams and hepatoscopy – divination by inspection of an animal's liver. Egypt was to make the art of dream interpretation its own, even as Rome was to take over hepatoscopy and turn it into a state religion. Babylon pursued its quest for wisdom via the stars, creating at length a system that was undoubtedly artificial and arbitrary but which was also balanced and satisfying.

Looking back over the long history of civilisation it seems as though all major advances have been as sudden steps rather than as slow evolutions. What has, in fact, happened, is that a quantitative change has abruptly become qualitative, the sum of many minor changes becoming dramatically evident. Some such sudden change is evident at an unknown period in Mesopotamia. Some time about the year 2000 BC someone in Babylon took the immense step that enabled him to view darkness and light not simply as the slow flapping of some gigantic wing but as the passage of one body around another. From that standpoint another step – not as dizzying in its extrapolation from one set of facts to another but still immensely impressive – took the embryonic astronomer to the point where he could deduce that the changing seasons were produced by the movement of one of these two bodies. Throughout, he would naturally be working on the common-sense assumption that it was the body upon which he was standing which was at rest while the other the blazing sun-god was moving, but this would not affect the truth of his observation.

With these two observations as basic data, he could then proceed to others – that there was a high and low point in both summer and winter and between the seasons themselves, the solstices and the equinoxes; that the passage of the sun shifted with the season but repeated itself year by year, forming the ecliptic.

These more sophisticated observations would then be linked to two very obvious details about the heavens which must have occurred to even the most primitive of creatures that could ever claim to be man : that the lunar orb changed twelve times a year and that five of the visible points of light in the sky were not fixed, but followed their own path. And a highly erratic path it seemed. Later, when the movement of these bodies could be plotted within the context of the solar system as a whole, it could be seen that they followed constant laws and paths. But at this remote period when they appeared only in the narrow band seen from the terrestrial surface, the movements appeared so erratic that the Babylonian astronomers referred to them as ' wild goats.' Later, the pithier Greek *planetes,* or wanderers, ousted the Babylonian phrase.

By about 1700 BC the astronomers had assembled the cast and the stage for their vast, aerial drama – the seven planets, counting sun and moon each as a planet in its own right; the sun's path around the earth; and, finally, the twelve sections of that path, the sections which also were ultimately to take a Greek name and be known as the Zodiac – ' pertaining to animals.'

A disappointment and puzzle which lies in wait for all youthful astronomers is the discovery that the signs of the Zodiac bear little or no resemblance to the constellations for which they stand as symbols. There are, in fact, two reasonably bright stars which stand out from the rest in Gemini and a reasonably free imagination could perhaps detect a crouching beast in Leo. But not the wildest exercise of imagination can find a centaur archer in Sagittarius, a female human in Virgo, a bull in Taurus and the rest.

The fact that it is virtually impossible to detect any coherent symbols in the constellations argues that it is highly unlikely that the names arise from the pattern of the constellations. A more likely explanation is that the symbols reflect some aspect of the seasons or even of weather. The first tentative mapping of the heavens may have had a religious significance, but it also had the valuable if humdrum virtue of providing a means of reckoning time for the farmer – a time to plant, a time to water, a time to reap. In this light, some at least of the symbols bear a possible common-sense interpretation, even if the majority remain wrapped in obscurity. Thus Libra, the Scales, can fairly be said to arise at the balance of the year when summer is on the point of giving way to autumn. Pisces and Aquarius occur in what would originally have been the rainy season. Other symbols probably arose from some real or fanciful aspect of the stars which occur in the constellation. Aries, the Ram, refers to its pre-eminent place in the Zodiac. The Babylonian year began when this constellation rose above the horizon and it was a perfectly natural step to associate this leader of the year with the leader of the flock – the ram.

How and why did this eminently practical farmer's calendar become transformed into an instrument for the foretelling of events? The answer may be among the tens of thousands of baked-clay tablets still lying buried in Mesopotamia but all that posterity has to go on are the chance references in Greek and Roman records. 'Chaldean' was, for them, actually synonymous with 'astrologer' but they were content to admire rather than investigate. It is neverthless possible to reconstruct the likely chain of events from the faint traces that they left.

The change took place in two great steps. The first was that in which the whole system was adapted away from its simple task of chronology to that of mapping the future on a general scale; the second marked the moment when interest in the individual's fate dominated interest in the fate of the state or the world at large. Both were linked to the concept of measuring time, a fact made clear when Greek ousted the ancient language, for ' horoscope ' means nothing more than a plan of time at a particular instant of the movement of the heavens.

The likelihood that the farmer's calendar would emerge as a precognitive instrument was inherent in its very purpose. It would take a mind of considerable sophistication to make a distinction between forecasting the likelihood of rain or drought in a given period ahead, and forecasting any other event, tangible or intangible. The observer would notice what was evident to the dullest intelligence : the stars were at once universal and constant. The planets weaving their way across this immutable backcloth must have resembled very closely the pattern of mortal affairs, making their transient mark against the immutable backcloth of the gods and of eternity. But the planets, erratic though their movements appeared, in fact followed discernible paths : laws could be deduced from them. Might it not therefore be possible to relate the movements of the planets to the affairs of men, so that if the one could be predicted, so could the other? Whether or not the question were asked in this specific manner it was in fact answered pragmatically. By about the year 2000 BC Babylonian astrologers were predicting human affairs on a broad scale – the so-called ' mundane astrology '.

By 600 BC this vague, tentative groping into the future had resolved itself into the precision of the personal horoscope. Among the thousands of cuneiform tablets which have been unearthed from the ruins of Babylon there is one, dated 234 BC, which might have been a horoscope extracted from a contemporary Sunday newspaper. The subject was a man with a Greek name, Aristokrates, who paid for a personal horoscope and received this very encouraging glimpse into his future :

The position of Jupiter means that his life will be regular. He will become rich and grow old. The position of Venus means that wherever he may go it will be favourable for him. Mercury and Gemini mean that he will have sons and daughters.

The instrument which could produce so detailed an analysis of Aristokrates' future was based upon a pseudo-precision. But it was consistent within its own framework and was thereafter to remain unchanged in its essentials. It was exported to China and to Egypt, to Greece and to Rome; it was to journey down the centuries, now exalted, now suppressed, surviving under fantastically different changes of manners and morals and beliefs. The symbols it gave the world were to become as common and as familiar as personal names : they were to appear on the twelfth-century cathedrals, on the Renaissance palaces of Italy, on nineteenth-century newspaper advertisements and finally, in the person of the Gemini spacecraft, return to the heavens whence they came.

How did this instrument come into being? It seems unlikely that that question ever will be answered. Something appears to have happened in Mesopotamia between approximately 2000 and 600 BC of which the Biblical Flood may be a folk-memory – something of a violence and a suddenness sufficient to destroy the civilisation on Crete and leave traces around the entire basin of the Eastern Mediterranean. In his *Worlds in Collision* Immanuel Velikovsky took the matter into the realm of science-fiction, postulating the birth of the planet Venus as the cause of a world-wide upheaval about 1500 BC. Whatever the cause of the disaster, certainly it effectively disrupted the transmission of tradition, throwing into what is likely to be permanent obscurity the causes of the emergence of the new skill. Velikovsky's theory is startling, drastic and possesses a number of rather large holes. But there is nothing inherently improbable in it – and much of it fills gaps that otherwise obstinately remain unfilled. The erratic behaviour of Venus before it settled down into its present orbit, is, in fact, recorded on one of the earliest surviving Babylonian tablets, the so-called Ammizaduga astronomical tablets, produced about the year 1600 BC. If, in addition, it could be assumed that Venus had indeed appeared as a new planet in the Babylonian skies some time before these Ammizaduga records then this would go a long way towards explaining the comparatively sudden appearance of the now familiar astrological system. A people already predisposed to regard the skies as a mirror of the future would have that predisposition enhanced by the appearance of a brilliant new ' wild goat,' grazing in the fields of heaven somewhere between the Earth and the Sun.

CENTRAL AND SOUTH AMERICA

Half a planet separates Babylon from the Americas, but greater by far than the distance of space is the distance of time. The 2,000 years which separate the Babylonians from the Aztecs mark a dizzying period in the world's history – the rise and fall of Rome and the empires to which, in turn, it gave birth; the rise and dominance of Christianity; the entry of a new, technologically oriented world; the spirit of experiment and the restless search for novelty; the awareness of a wider world with, paradoxically, the knowledge that the parent earth was but one, and that of the smallest, in a family attendant upon the sun. All this was to occur between the fall of Babylon and the fall of Tenochtitlan. But despite the gulf of time and manners and space between the two cultures there yet exists a curious correspondence, a similarity of means and purpose which the observer can do no more than record without attempt at explanation as to how it came about.

The Assyrians apart, the Aztecs were undoubtedly the most bloodthirsty civilisation ever to have raised itself up out of primitive chaos. At the birth of a baby boy its mother whispered a prayer over it which must have chilled any other woman even to contemplate. ' Your duty is to give the sun the blood of your enemies to drink, and to feed the earth with their corpses.' Habitually, they engaged in mock battles whose sole purpose was to obtain living sacrifices for the altar stone. Yet this same ferocious, courageous, people fell passive victim to a tiny handful of hungry Spaniards.

Their basic will to resist had been eroded even before the Spaniards set foot upon the land. Some two to three years before Cortes set sail, the Aztecs recorded an extraordinary crop of ill-omened signs – a comet, monsters seen in the streets by day, armed men in the skies. A circumstantial tale was told of how the emperor Montezuma ordered that a large and splendid new sacrificial stone should be brought for the embellishment of his capital. His officers found the desired stone – but it had been granted the gift of speech, pitying them and upbraiding their master. ' Poor wretches, why do you labour in vain?' it demanded as they toiled and sweated to carry it back with them. ' I will never arrive in Mexico. Go, tell Montezuma that it is too late. He should have sent for me before. Now he no longer needs me for a terrible event is about to happen.' In Tenochtitlan itself an exotic bird, wearing a mirror upon its head, was captured and brought to the emperor. Peering into the mirror he saw a sight never seen before in the Americas, a sight which literally he lacked the words to describe for he was looking at men mounted upon beasts. All these signs were interpreted by the priests as being related to an event supposed to take place in the year one-reed – the year when Quetzalcoatal, the exiled god-king would return. In the Christian calendar the year one-reed was 1519; and it was in 1519 that Hernando Cortes sailed from Cuba and landed in Tabasco at the head of 553 men and leading sixteen horses.

If Babylon was a star-struck civilisation, then the civilisation of Central and Southern America was obsessed by time. Olmec, Toltec, Maya and Aztec – each contributed some unique aspect to the culture of the peninsula; but each, too, showed an extraordinary preoccupation with the calendar.

Mayan hieroglyphics remain as enigmatic as the hieroglyphics of the Etruscans but sufficient of the developed Mayan astronomy passed into the historic Aztec culture, if in a debased form, to allow at least an educated guess at the cycle of the time-based religion. Significantly, perhaps, both Maya and Aztec regarded the planet Venus as a destroyer, a dark and bloody hunter of the skies, an identification which may perhaps be linked to the theory of the newborn planet devastating the world by its approaches and retreats on an erratic orbit.

The Mayan/Aztec calendar was one of 365 days, falling just short of the solar year. The astronomers were perfectly well aware of this and, in correcting it, created an extra-ordinary ceremony which was eventually to permeate the religion. When the sum of the error had reached a predeter-mined quantity, the priests announced, and may have believed, that the world was ending. Life could continue only by sacrifice to the gods and therefore, at the critical moment, the priests ascended the summit of the temple – a temple that was virtually an artificial hill – and there awaited the rising of the Pleiades. As soon as the constellation had passed the mid-heaven a fire was kindled in the gaping breast of a newly-killed victim and as the smoke and flame arose so the continuity of life was proclaimed and celebrated. This extra-ordinary ceremony may contain an explanation for the abandoning of Mayan cities in what is now Honduras and Yucatan. Archaeology provides no clue as to the reason for the abandonment: there is no trace of fire or flood, of enemy action, of drought or any natural hazard. The probability is that the city had come to the end of its predicted life cycle and, in obedience to that fact, its citizens walked out of it. It was an extreme result of the influence that time and the stars had upon a highly civilised, highly intelligent people. Ultimately, that influence was to prove fatal as the Aztecs unnerved, watched at last in reality what they believed had been so long mirrored in the heavens.

ISRAEL

Hebrew literature is probably the richest in concrete imagery of any of the world's great literatures. The immense impact of the Bible owes in part to this fact, for generation after generation among races wholly alien to that of its authors could grasp the essentials through the veil of translation. Rock, fire, bread, water, bone, hand, foot – it was with the words for the tangible universe that the Hebrew prophets wove their net to catch the intangible. It is therefore significant that in this rich tapestry of concrete imagery the words for star, planet, and the rest occur with comparative infrequency. Although they were close neighbours to the Babylonians, shared with them much of their traditions, were oppressed by them, alternatively hated and admired them – despite this close correspondence of activities they paid only a passing attention to the dominant Babylonian talent – astronomy and its derivative astrology. In both Old and New Testament overt astrological references could almost be numbered on the fingers of one hand. Outstanding, towering above all others is the Journey of the Magi whose star was, probably, a garbled reference to the drawing up of a horoscope. If this interpretation is correct then the three Wise Men from the East were not following a literally moving star but rather going to a place earlier indicated by that star in a horoscope. Elsewhere, references to the stars as divinatory or active elements are meagre and unimportant. 'They fought from heaven, the stars in their courses fought against Sisera', celebrates the destruction of Assyria. Amos elsewhere charges his men to 'Seek him that maketh the seven stars in Orion and turneth the shadow of death into the morning'. There is little enough here compared with the wealth of stargazing imagery in the annals of their neighbours and late oppressors.

The Babylonian astrologer was, if anything, a scientist. His premise might be mistaken but his technique could hardly be faulted for he, too, was attempting to draw up constant laws from observed phenomena. The Hebrew prophet was, if anything, a poet, moved spontaneously to pronounce upon this or that aspect of existence. Tradition has limited his role largely to the ability to look into the future. Strictly speaking, that ability was virtually irrelevant to his overriding function – acting as a communication channel between the Creator and his creatures. The Creator being, by definition, omniscient then knowledge of the future was included in his communications, but only as a byproduct. Even the Greek translators who turned the Hebrew *nabir* into the familiar *prophet* recognised that fact for *prophetes* itself simply means he who speaks forth.

The earliest reference to prophets in Israel precisely illustrated their nature. In the book of Samuel the story is told of how Saul met a band of prophets who were in an ecstasy, an ecstasy which communicated itself to Saul so that he stripped himself naked and remained in a trance for over twenty-four hours. The ancient Hebrew prophet resembled the modern Muslim dervish – in particular that class known variously as the whirling dervish or the dancing dervish – a person who can, by certain techniques, induce in himself a species of trance or hysteria. The technique is also apparent in those fundamentalist Christian sects where, following rhythmic chanting, stamping and clapping, certain members of the congregation burst into the gibberish known as the ' speaking in tongues '.

This trance-suspension occurs again and again in the accounts of the prophets. In *Kings* is told how Elijah ran the entire way from Mount Carmel to Jezreel in front of Ahab's chariot – a feat that would have been impossible to an ordinary man in a normal frame of mind. The prophet came to be looked upon as a magician who could bring rain in a period of drought, food in a period of famine and could even bring the dead to life. His very garments and possessions were regarded as sharing his divine powers : the 'mantle of Elijah' was no mere metaphor but an exact statement of

c

belief – that he who possessed the garment would also inherit the prophet's abilities.

The belief that ecstatic prophecy was, in effect, contagious, found expression in the fact that prophets tended to live together in loose associations or guilds. They shared the same house, ate communally, divided their possessions between each other. In a sense they must have resembled the monastery of a later period, for each guild or household had its head. But essentially they were equals and independents, living together for the sake of convenience and mutual support but bound by no inflexible rules. From these communal homes they ranged out over the country singly or in groups, exhorting, accusing, ' speaking forth.' Sometimes the king might wait upon them, but more often it was they who appeared before the king, erupting out of the desert and the wilderness to excoriate in burning language. Sometimes, under the pressure of religious emotion, their language passes the barrier of common meaning, bearing as it were a double load of significance. In particular, their passionate desire for nationhood – a desire in which it is impossible to isolate the political from the religious elements – formed a nucleus for the preaching of the coming of the Messiah, the ideal king through whom could be effected reconciliation with God. How much these prophecies were wishful-thinking, how much allegories and how much a cloudy foreshadowing it is impossible to say. But by a quirk of history these ' prophecies ' were to survive and flourish as an indestructible part of the heritage of the West while those of their colleagues belonging to far wealthier, far more powerful races, were to be forgotten.

Chapter 3
The Classical World

Greece placed the final imprint upon astrology – but did so almost as an afterthought. For astrology came late to Greece – more than a thousand years after the archaic inhabitants of the land had evolved a complex system of oracles which became part of the true religion of the people. The antics of Zeus and Hera, of Ares and Aphrodite were tales to be told: the pronouncements of Delphi were listened to eagerly and obeyed unquestioningly – where they could be understood.

The Greek and Hebrew mind could not have been more different one from the other, but there was one matter in which there was, curiously, a close correspondence. The Hebrew prophet and the Greek oracle resembled each other far more closely than would be expected from their different approach to religion. The wise men of other races – the Chaldeans, the Egyptians, the Romans – tended to use more or less mechanical means in order to divine the future or the wishes of the gods. The Hebrew and the Greek spoke direct, after placing themselves in a type of trance.

Superficially, the culture of Greece appears to be a luminous joyous experience, concerned with the realities of flesh and stone and sunlight. But beneath that cheerfully pagan appearance there was a dark stratum. Achilles summed it up when, anguished, he cried out to Odysseus, who had braved hell to visit him, ' Better to be the slave of the meanest

peasant on Earth than to be king of all the dead.' Life went
on beyond the grave, but in a dreary and joyless manner
which no man in his senses could desire. And before the grave
was reached, each man's path was clearly mapped out for him.
As in Christian theology, that concept of predestination clashed
with the concept of free will and, again just as in Christianity,
the clash was never resolved. The same people who created
the delicate balance of democracy, a way of life dependent
upon the continual exercise of individual responsibility, also
created the macabre picture of the blind Fates and, behind
them, the avenging Furies ready to pounce upon those who
transgressed the dictates of gods, and the gods were themselves
caught up in this vast web and chain of circumstances. The
working out of fate provided material for drama which, even
in the wholly alien world of the twentieth century, yet strikes
a universal note. Orestes slew his mother Clytemnestra and
therefore had to be punished: but his mother slew his father
and therefore it was his duty to avenge his father's death. Who
was to blame? Not even, perhaps, Clytemnestra who would
not have taken a lover and therefore slain her husband if her
husband had not gone to Troy. Could one blame the gods?
Not really. Ultimately, all that the Greek could do was to
shrug and say, This is the way of things, and illustrate, not
explain.

Caught up as they were between the concept of a blind and
merciless fate, and the nagging belief that man was, despite
all evidence to the contrary, responsible for at least part of his
actions, the Greeks sought a possible way out by throwing the
burden back onto the shoulders of the Fates. Cleromancy –
divination by lot – became not only a part of religion but an
indispensable part of politics. Candidates for office were chosen
by drawing coloured beans from a bag or by throwing specially
chosen stones in another system known as lithology. It was
even known to resolve a matter of public policy or a law case
by such means but when important matters were put to the
chance of lottery, the actual throwing of the stones or with-

4 The oracle of Apollo at Delphi : King Aegeus of Athens consults the Pythia, fifth century BC

5 Coin showing Augustus' birth-sign of Capricorn. The beast is controlling a rudder attached to a globe, symbolising Rome's global rule

6 Seeking auguries from the entrails of a bull, second century AD

drawing of the beans was entrusted only to a professional prophetess, and the most important of all were referred to one of the three oracles of Greece, that of Dodona, Delphi or Olympia.

Delphi, Apollo's own oracle, was the most famous of the three. It stood in a superb setting, the focal point of a vast natural amphitheatre whose background was Mount Parnassus. To one side was the terrible gorge of Pleistus, to the other the town with Apollo's temple dominating it. The oracle itself was in a cave, through which ran a sacred stream and at whose very centre stood the *omphalos,* the navel or centre of the Earth.

Plutarch, writing in the second century AD, stated that the cave was found by accident at least six hundred years before his time. In the cave was a cleft through which some kind of gas – probably sulphur – issued in a regular stream. The gas gave convulsions to a number of goats who were grazing nearby, and also affected the goatherd when he went to their rescue. During his seizure or fit he was apparently in a light trance, uttering words which were individually clear but, taken together, seemed meaningless. Plutarch was drawing upon legends and half-remembered, distorted facts. The basis of his story is probably accurate, but exactly how the chance-discovered cave became the centre of a cult spread throughout the civilised world cannot even be conjectured. By the time it had achieved its international fame writers both hostile and sympathetic left a clear enough account of the means and ritual by whereby the greatest of all oracles made its pronouncements.

The prophet was always a woman – the Pythia. In the early period she had to be a virgin, of noble birth and of good appearance, but these qualifications were hastily revised when a Pythia was seduced in the sacred cave itself. Thereafter she had to be at least fifty and good looks were, if anything, a disqualification.

Consulting the Delphic oracle was an expensive affair and

it was no accident that the majority of the Delphic records refer to kings, princes and wealthy cities who could afford the treasure of gold and silver deemed to be fitting ' presents ' for the god. The charitable element in all religions, however, later gave the poor a chance at Delphi when, annually, the Pythia would leave the sanctuary and sit on the temple steps when all who wished could put a question to her.

The Pythia gave a consultation once a month on average. After having been ritually purified she was escorted into the chamber where stood the *omphalos*. There a goat was sprinkled with holy water and, if it shivered in a prescribed manner, the auspices were deemed favourable. The Pythia was then dressed in her sacred robe, crowned with the laurel, Apollo's plant, and descended deep down into the sanctuary where she breathed in the vapours and chewed bay leaves, probably to increase the hallucinogenic action. Incense was burnt and then, seated on a tripod, the Pythia waited the visitation of the god. Near her would be the priest of Apollo whose task it was to interpret the enigmatic message for the client who would usually be waiting outside the sanctuary.

Apollonius of Tyana, himself a prophet – or conjurer – of no small ability, described a visit he paid to Delphi which testified to the effect he had on a not particularly impressionable man. He was allowed right into the *adytum,* the sanctuary itself.

> Its walls are decorated with the rich offerings which attest the truth of the oracles and the gratitude of those consultants who have been favoured by fate. At first we had difficulty in seeing anything, for the burning incense and other perfumes filled the place with dense smoke. Behind the statue of the god is the crypt into which one descends by a gradual slope, but the servants of the temple keep the consultants far enough away from the Pythia to make their presence unnoticeable.

The oracle gave Apollonius an unfavourable reading – he had

asked if he would be remembered after death and the Pythia replied that he would indeed be remembered, but with obloquy. He destroyed the piece of papyrus on which the prediction was written but had the grace to remark ' That is what all consultants do whose pride has not been satisfied.'

Delphi survived for an extraordinarily long period. It was consulted and honoured for at least eight hundred years and, even after its fame had become tarnished, its prophecies inaccurate, pilgrims still made the long, hard and expensive journey to that cave in the great sweep of the hills. The very fact that its power waned, the very fact that its prophecies became inaccurate argues that, at one period, the oracle at Delphi possessed some quality not detectable by normal means. The quality may have been caused by the fumes emerging from the bowels of the earth; it may have been a product of the bay leaves combined with sulphur – but it existed for long enough and unequivocally enough for a sceptic such as Cicero to say, ' Never could the oracle of Delphi have been so overwhelmed with so many important offerings from monarchs and nations if all the ages had not proved the truth of its oracles.' The powerful men who made rich gifts to the temple were not taking part in a religious act of vague and general propitiation but virtually a commercial transaction in which they paid out hard cash for information about a future event. If the ratio of success to failure had been the ordinary one of pure chance, it seems unlikely, to say the least, that caravans laden with gold and silver and precious spices and perfumes would have continued to wind their way over the tortuous roads to the shrine.

' The God of Delphi neither reveals, nor conceals, but hints ', Heraclitus the philosopher stated. The fragmentary prophecies resemble the cautious pronouncements of mediums – even more, the elliptical, highly metaphorical vocabulary of Nostradamus. The lack of any bibliographical or chronological check makes it impossible to determine with any real degree of accuracy whether or no the predictions were made before they were fulfilled. But a sufficient number of responsible writers have firmly maintained that they were and, accepting these pronouncements, posterity is driven to find some plausible explanation. As with Nostradamus, the overwhelming impression given is not that the oracle was deliberately concealing and hedging its bets, but rather as though the seer was aware only of vague colours and moving forms. It is as though the Pythia were looking, quite literally, as into a glass darkly. Thus, when the inhabitants of the island of Siphnos sent to ask whether their prosperity would continue, the oracle replied that it would do so until their market place and communal palace became white. They would then endure an ambush of wood which would be heralded by something or someone in red. The Siphnians, whose prosperity was founded on their gold and silver mines, eventually gilded the entire front of the communal palace and the buildings around the main square. The effect of this, in the dazzling Mediterranean sun, would indeed be as though the buildings had turned white. Equally certainly, it attracted pirates – men in wooden ships whose great ramming beaks were painted red for luck. It seems almost inescapable that the Pythia did indeed see something, but so vaguely, so amorphously as to give little value to her client.

The decline of the oracle set in by the second century AD. The Romans, energetic in this as in all other things, tried to restore its glory by degrees but, that failing, plundered it in a mixture of piety and cupidity. The emperor Julian the Apostate swore to re-establish it and asked how he should go about it, but received, in reply, the last prediction of the oracle – its day was done and it would not again be revived.

The fact that Delphi's swo sister oracles – that at Dodona and at Olympia – underwent a decline at approximately the same period shows that the causes were as much external as internal. It was at this period, too, that astrology swept through Greece : the oracle, the direct voice of the god, gave ground to the stars, the mirror of an unchangeable and impersonal Fate. It was a Greek, Lucian of Samosata, who made the first clear defence of astrology:

> If it is admitted that a horse in gallop, that birds in flying and men in walking make the stones jump or drive the little floating particles of dust by the wind of their course, why should you deny that the stars have any effect? The smallest fire sends us its emanations, and although it is not for us that the stars burn, and they care very little about warning us, why should we not receive any emanations from them? Astrology, it is true, cannot make that good which is evil. It can effect no change in the course of events, but it renders a service to those who cultivate it by announcing to them great things to come: it produces joy by anticipation at the same time that if fortifies them against evil.

Astrology entered Greece through two quite different channels: directly from Babylon, supposedly via the Chaldean priest Berosus who set up a school on the island of Cos in the third century BC, and from Alexandria. The effect of its impact upon Greece could be measured by the fact that now, for the first time, the planets were given personal names. Hitherto they had been merely identified by their appearance, but the Babylonians had long since identified them with one or other of the gods. Nabu, Ishtar, Nergal, Marduk and Ninib, such were the outlandish names with which the Greeks first struggled and then substituted their own elegant versions – Hermes, Aphrodite, Ares, Zeus, Kronos.

Three centuries before astrology superseded the oracles in Greece, however, the great mathematician Pythagoras had placed his highly distinctive imprint upon the whole concept of the movement of the heavens. In his work, and that of his followers, was displayed that indissoluble symbiosis of art and science and religion which marked the thought of his day. Pythagoras began by seeking a rational picture of the universe and ended by creating a philosophy which was indistinguishable from a religion. The Babylonian view of the universe had been totally earthbound: the world was conceived as resting in a kind of pan or container. Overhead was the fixed dome of heaven, supported by ramparts; beneath was a chamber of water.

Pythagoras maintained the earth at the centre: even his mind could not yet make the great leap, although one of his disciples did daringly postulate the existence of a 'central fire' around which the planets moved. But in place of the squat, flat earth in its covered pan, Pythagoras substituted the beautiful simplicity of the sphere surrounded by other spheres. Each of these bodies was affixed to a vast crystal sphere, the outer enclosing the inner and, because each moved at a different speed, each was supposed to emit a note at a different pitch. This was the 'music of the spheres', the Pythagorean scale in which all the notes blended into one pure, harmonious sound.

The Pythagorean universe appealed to the aesthete and the rationalist as much as the philosopher. It demonstrated conclusively that the universe was a whole whose parts satisfyingly interlocked one with the other. It explained the apparent movement of the planets and the course of the seasons. It also, incidentally, placed astronomy in a strait-jacket for a millenium and more, so geometrically perfect and satisfying was its form. In 300 BC Aristarchus of Samos actually postulated a heliocentric system, with the earth itself not only moving around the sun but also revolving on its own axis. But so preposterous was the theory, so outrageously did it contradict all rational evidence that its author was mocked and his creation ignored.

EGYPT

After the fall of Babylon, in 538 BC, astrology went into a profound decline. It would have been rational, indeed, to have predicted its total disappearance for Greece was still absorbed in the oracular tradition and Egypt had evolved a tradition

of magic that could not have been far removed from char-
latanry. Certainly Herodotus, writing in the fifth century BC,
was scathing about the Egyptian ' mysteries ' with their talking
statues and stage-managed ceremonies. The favourite Egyptian
technique of divination was oneiromancy – the revealing of
the future through dreams. The dream was believed to be a
direct transmission either from a god, or the spirit of a dead
person. The more dedicated dreamers would actually sleep
upon a grave, hoping thereby to be closer to the source of the
transmission. Egyptian records abound with stories of dreams
and their interpretations but the most famous of all was
transmitted to posterity via the literature of a subject people.
Joseph's interpretation of the Pharaoh's dream of seven fat
and seven lean cattle and seven thick and seven thin ears of
corn might have been no more than a lucky shot. Equally, as
a responsible minister, he might have taken advantage of his
master's vivid but meaningless dream in order to make
economic provision for the future.

It was in Egypt, in the great intellectual clearing house of
Alexandria, that there was developed between the second and
first centuries BC, two bodies of occult works which were to
have a remarkably long life when exported to wholly different
environments. The first was the proto-astrological work attributed to the Pharaoh Nechepso and his priest Petosiris.
Nechepso was a purely legendary figure but Petosiris probably
existed in reality, for there was an Egyptian philosopher of
that name who wrote extensively on Greek theology. *The
Revelations of Nechepso and Petosiris* were supposed to have
been the secrets revealed by Petosiris after studying the stars,
secrets which were naturally passed on to the Pharaoh as
high priest. They were, in effect, a corruption – or an enrich-
ment – of classic Chaldean astrology and their appearance in
Alexandria was to be the herald of a new development in
astrology.

At about the same time there first appeared in manuscript
form the body of occult lore known as the books of Hermes

Trismegistus. Hermes was the Greek equivalent of the god Thoth, traditionally associated with occult learning and, hence, with astrology. Trismegistus meant, simply, the Thrice-Great and the body of Hermetical writings was a compendium or encyclopaedia built up from the immense library at Alexandria. Later, dim memories of that incredible storehouse turned the compilers of the compendium into legendary figures, identifying them totally with Hermes. Paradoxically, while the human scribes were elevated to an almost god-like status, the god himself was reduced to mortality. It was believed that his dead body was found, in a cave, some time after the Flood with, near it, a precious tablet of emerald upon which were engraved the most valuable extracts from the 20,000 books he was supposed to have written during his life.

The Hermetical compendium contained the secrets of alchemy as well as astrology and medicine. It outlined, for the first time, that ' Zodiacal Man ' which was to dominate European medicine throughout the Middle Ages and Renaissance. Essentially, the Zodiacal Man was the product of correspondences, the attempt to relate the appearance of one thing to the meaning of another, in itself a version of the Pythagorean concept of the unity of things. Thus, man's body was specifically and exactly compared with the planet upon which he moved and had his being:

> The macrocosm has animals, terrestrial and aquatic: in the same way man has fleas, lice, and tapeworms. The macrocosm has rivers, springs and seas: man has intestines. The macrocosm has sun and moon: man has two eyes, the right related to the sun, the left to the moon. The macrocosm has the twelve signs of the Zodiac: man contains them, too, from his head namely from the Ram, to his feet, which correspond to the Fish.

The Zodiac was again rising in the consciousness of man after having been below his horizon for nearly three centuries.

7 The theory of correspondence showing Aries and assumed
human counterpart

The mythical Hermes Trismegistus infused magic into the
Chaldean system. The very real Claudius Ptolemy drew
together into one logical whole elements of astrological theory
which had been evolved over many centuries and in widely
differing places, combining Pythagoras with Hermes Trismegistus, Chaldean with Greece and Egypt, to create the system
which, with basic changes, is that which is recognised as
' astrology ' today.

Ptolemy, although living and working centuries before the
' scientist ' was recognised as being a different kind of thinker,
belonged to a type which would be perhaps more at home in
the twentieth than the second century AD. Essentially his was
the type of mind which believes that if only sufficient information is accumulated and classified then a pattern must emerge
and an answer must be produced. Ptolemy was probably
more industrious than brilliant, a compiler rather than an
innovator, but he placed the post-medieval world heavily in
his debt. His great book *Geography* consisted, for the most
part, of topographical information drawn up by, and for the

convenience of, travellers throughout the Roman Empire. But, furnished with the coordinates which he provided for each place mentioned, it was sufficient to create, in the fifteenth century, the first rational map of the world that had been seen since the fall of the Empire. The *Astronomy*, too, was largely a compilation of other men's work but served to give the Renaissance world an objective picture of the universe and a reasonably accurate picture of the earth's place in it.

The *Tetrabiblos* performed the same function for astrology : as far as Ptolemy was concerned the effect of the stars on human destiny was as real, as undisputable as their presence in the skies. Even as he conceived it his duty to provide his readers with a picture of the world in space, so he conceived it his duty to provide a picture of the world in time, the future. Basically, he postulated an all-embracing substance or influence, which he termed the Ambient, through which extraterrestrial influences were transmitted. These influences were not only psychic but also physical, the stars being capable of causing floods, droughts and storms as well as affecting the seasons.

The planets fell into one of two classes, malevolent or benevolent, and each possessed, in addition, certain attributes of heat or cold, wetness or dryness. 'The ancients', he wrote, ' accepted two of the planets, Venus and Jupiter, together with the Moon as beneficent because they abound in the hot and the moist and Saturn and Mars as producing effects of the opposite nature, one because of his excessive cold and the other for his excessive dryness '. From this it was a short step to that dogma of ' correspondences ' which is the leitmotif of astrology. Confidently he applied the theory to nations as well as to individuals : thus, those who lived in countries looking towards the east were open and honest by nature, ' for in all their characteristics they are principally conformed to the sun's nature '. He followed the Hermetic writers in assigning each part of the body to a particular star or planet, a fact which was to have immense significance in medieval medicine. And finally he laid down the laws for determining genethliacal horoscopes – personal horoscopes based on the moment of birth. He raised – but dodged – the problem which was to embarrass astrologers throughout the coming centuries. The most important formative influence must surely occur at the moment of conception, rather than birth but while few people ever knew the exact hour of their birth, none could possibly know the hour of conception. Later astrologers were to adopt the convenient Egyptian explanation that, at the hour of birth, the Moon would infallibly be in the same sign as that which was in the ascendant at the hour of conception.

ROME

The records of prophecy in Rome are inextricably entangled with politics. Hindsight makes it seem more than likely that the most famous prophecy of all, that of Vestritius Spurinna to Caesar to 'Beware the Ides of March' was a leakage, deliberate or otherwise, of the plot to kill him. But it was most circumstantial in its details. As Suetonius was later to transmit the story :

> The impending death of Caesar was announced by the most patent of omens. A few months earlier the colonists of Capua, who had emigrated thither in consequence of the Julian laws, came in the course of their building operations upon prehistoric graves. These they opened with all the more alacrity owing to the fact that they found in them many vessels of ancient craftsmanship. In the monument that served as a tomb for Capys, the founder of Capua, they discovered a bronze tablet bearing the inscription in Greek : ' When once the houses of Capys are brought to light, then a branch of the Julian house will be slain by the hand of one of his kindred. His death, however, will soon be avenged by terrible consequences in Italy.'

Caesar believed implicitly in astrology even if he held a suspended judgement regarding the value of the more traditional methods of Roman divination. It is therefore curious that he paid no attention to Spurinna's warning, whether it were delivered as a result of political or prophetic foreknowledge. The incident was an excellent example of the dilemma which faced any politician who relied, whether out of personal or official conviction, upon the utterance of prophets. If the prophet's dictum clashed with the politician's – which should he follow? Caesar apparently decided that the political advantages to be gained by going to the Forum on that particular day far outweighed the rather cloudy warnings of danger – a fact upon which his enemies relied. The later story of how his wife Calpurnia tried to dissuade him after her dream in which she saw their houses collapsing and himself dead in her arms was almost certainly a later embellishment. And it was probably from this embellishment that Suetonius later elaborated his own, more complex story. But nothing in the account of the death of Julius Caesar would have struck his contemporaries as being particularly unusual. The Romans, whom posterity was to laud or berate as the ultimate in hard-headed common sense, ran both their private and their public lives on the firm assumption that the future could be seen as clearly as the present or the past.

In the matter of prophecy, at least, Rome drew little from either Greece or Egypt. In the later, lusher days of the Caesars, when strange Oriental religions and customs were imported into Italy and flourished during the long years of decadence, Egyptian astrologers and other soothsayers were to jostle with each other. But in the great days of the Republic, the Roman looked back to a more or less indigenous breed of prophet for their own needs. These were the prophets of Etruria – the Haruspices.

The trade of the haruspex was probably Babylonian in origin for its primary technique was hepatoscopy, the examination of an animal's liver, which had dominated in Mesopotamia before being overshadowed by astrology. Baby-

Ionian medicine had regarded the liver, rather than the heart or even the brain, as being the most vital organ of the body. Tyros were trained with clay models, each of which was clearly marked with the characteristics for which the students were to seek in the real thing. The shape, the number of lobes, the condition, the quantity, colour and quality of the blood, each had something vital to say to the Babylonian baru, or seer. Hepatoscopy was kept firmly in the hands of the great, in the earlier centuries. Only the king and the nobles of his immediate entourage were allowed to take part in the solemn ceremony when the animal was killed, its liver extracted and placed upon the god's altar.

In Babylon, hepatoscopy declined in importance. In the latter years ' reading ' the intestines of sheep edged out pure hepatoscopy before the aesthetically and intellectually more pleasing art of astrology dominated the whole field of prophecy. The messy butcher's technique never found much favour in Greece, but Rome adopted it wholeheartedly whether it came direct from Babylon or via the Etruscans. Increased medical knowledge, in particular that unfolded in the natural history of Pliny, served to draw the Roman's attention to the heart as well as the liver. The haruspices were always Etruscan, and never Roman by birth, the Romans themselves seemed to look upon them with a divided mind, half respectfully, half contemptuously. Cato remarked that he wondered how one haruspex could look another in the face without laughing : haruspices were ranked considerably lower than augurs, the official soothsayers, and their art was never formally part of the state religion. But there was a regular college of sixty haruspices in Rome and the practitioners were accorded, in the popular mind, all the respect due to priests.

The animal – usually an ox – had to be entirely without blemish and was dedicated to the god whose favour was sought. It may very well have been drugged beforehand, for most seem to have taken part in the ceremony with rather remarkable docility. Despatched by a pole-axe and its throat

D

cut, the technique was to extract the liver or other desired organ while the animal was still, in effect, alive, that is, the blood was still coursing through its body. A dried up and shrivelled liver was regarded as the worst of all possible omens, but it was not enough for the organ to be simply in a healthy condition. In addition to the same qualities which the Babylonian seers had sought there was added, in the later days of the Republic, the complication of relating the shape and size of the liver to astrology. Models of the liver were made marked as for a horoscope and, with this added refinement, the haruspex claimed to be able to predict for individuals as well as for the state.

Astrology entered Rome during the last decades of the Republic and, like other lusher elements, was destined to flourish under the Caesars like some monstrous plant. The first clearly identified astrologer was Publius Nigidius Figulus who, in the traditional manner, was able to combine that cloudy career with that of mathematician, historian and, to a lesser degree, politician. It was this last activity which enabled him to make a prophecy which established his name for posterity, at least. At the meeting of the Senate a certain senator, Octavius by name, arrived late, breathless and apologetic. His wife had just given birth to a son, he announced. Nigidius promptly rose to his feet in the Senate and congratulated Octavius. ' You have given us a master', he said. ' And not only us, but the world.' Octavius' son was to be better known to history as Augustus. According to the historian Dio Cassius, Octavius was by no means pleased with the news. As a good republican, he conceived it his duty promptly to rid Rome of that particular threat but Nigidius dissuaded him from infanticide, with a profound effect upon the future history of Rome.

Whatever the truth of Dio Cassius' story, Augustus was certainly deeply impressed by astrologers and soothsayers. He was most influenced by a certain Theogenes who allegedly prophesied the precise circumstances of his assumption to imperial power. Theogenes belonged as much to the old race of soothsayer as to the fashionable new breed of astrologer but Augustus was sufficiently moved to have a silver medal struck bearing his birth-sign of Capricorn. Later, as emperor, he was to give that motif a far wider currency, first by commissioning a superb cameo and later by stamping it upon a coin of his reign.

The flattering biographers of the emperors invariably introduced an element of the miraculous into their work, drawing attention to some omen or portent which had been heaven's indication of the future of their subject. Augustus, reigning during the lifetime of Christ, was a natural object of Christian hagiographers, intent upon proving the divine fore-shadowing of this or that aspect of their creed. At the height of his power he built an enormous temple to Peace and then, so the story ran, consulted the Tiburtine Sibyl as to how long the building and, hence, the Roman peace would last. ' Until a virgin gives birth to a child ' was the enigmatic answer which the emperor not unnaturally interpreted as meaning for per-petuity. The temple collapsed in the year which was to be known as AD 1. A similar legend grew up around his con-sultation with the same Sibyl in which he asked whether he should accept the title ' God of the nations ' that a canny Senate had offered him. She gave him the customary devious answer which he interpreted favourably and then, prompted by some unknown unease, he asked her if any greater than he would ever be born. Her answer was, for once, unequivocal. It happened that the consultation was taking place, on the Palatine, late at night and, as the Emperor finished his question, a meteor flared across the sky. ' That is the sign you ask ', she said. ' One world has ended and another begun. A child has just been born who is the king of future millenia.' Thereafter she proceeded to describe, in impressive detail, the circumstances of the birth and role of Christ.

Curiously, it was during Augustus' reign that Rome was almost swept free of astrologers and professional prophets on the Emperor's personal orders. Given his personal belief in their efficacy, the explanation for the purge is probably political; he considered it only too likely that an ambitious man who had been encouraged by a favourable prediction would attempt to make it come true.

The prohibition continued under Tiberius, Augustus' successor, with increased and increasing severity. Both astrologer and client were liable to be tortured and executed if discovered. Tiberius' belief in the powers of astrology were as firm as Augustus' : indeed, habitually he had the horoscopes cast for all potential rivals. It was a potent extension of his rule through fear, for there were few, if any, astrologers who would have resisted the emperor's suggestion that such an element might very likely be found in a given person's horoscope. Yet, according to Suetonius, one fortunate astrologer not only survived a session with the emperor but made his fortune. The man was Thrasyullus, who was summoned to Capri to cast certain horoscopes for the emperor. The main ascent to Tiberius' most curious pleasure villa was via a narrow path which wound its way up the face of a cliff. Visitors to the emperor were attended by a gigantic black slave, part of whose duties were to nudge unwelcome visitors over the edge of the path.

Thrasyullus arrived at the villa safely and discharged his duty. The emperor then asked him, casually, to erect his own horoscope and waited impassively while Thrasyullus did so. And what do you see in it, he demanded when the astrologer had completed his task. In terror, Thrasyullus replied that he foresaw the imminence of his own death. The emperor congratulated him : it was his habit to dispose of the astrologer he had consulted in order that the victim whose horoscope had been erected should not be warned. Thrasyullus' fate was to have been edged off the path by the slave on their return down to the harbour, he informed the trembling man. But he had shown himself to be not only a good astrologer but also an honest man and, with the caprice of the great, Tiberius loaded

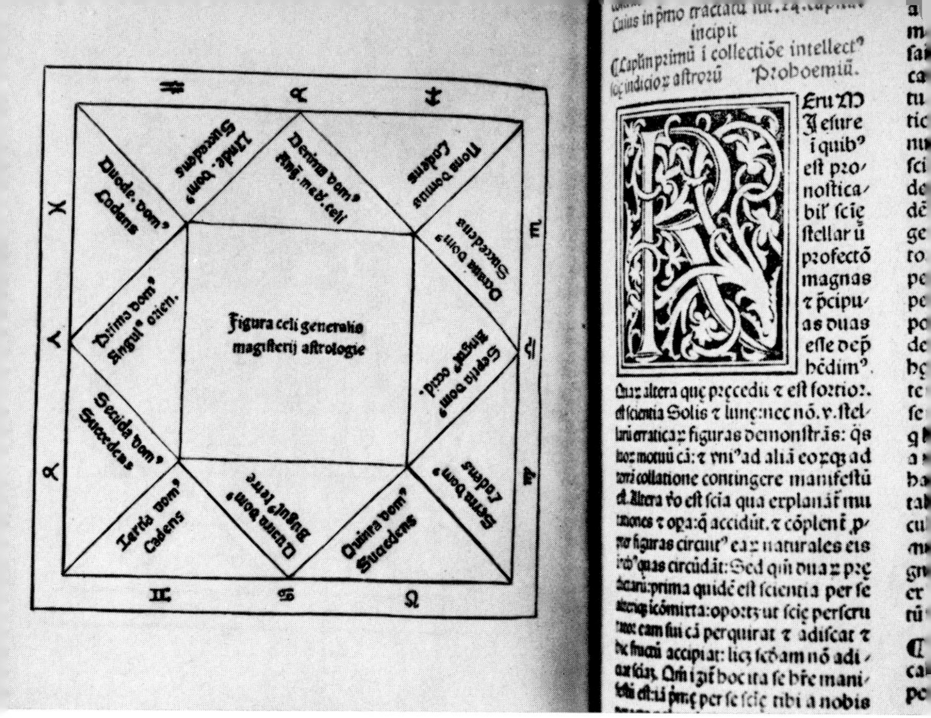

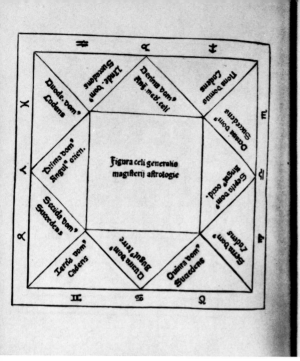

The horoscope figure contains the following labels:

Figura celi generalis magisterij astrologie

Decima Dom⁹ Fins medi celi
Vndecima Dom⁹ Cadens
Duodecima Dom⁹ Succedens
Octaua Dom⁹ Succedens
Prima Dom⁹ Angul orient.
Nona Dom⁹ Cadens
Septima Dom⁹ Angul occd.
Secuda Dom⁹ Succedens
Sexta Dom⁹ Cadens
Tertia Dom⁹ Cadens
Quarta Dom⁹ Angul Terre
Quinta Dom⁹ Succedens

The adjacent printed text column reads:

Caius in pmo tractatu sui .ca. capitulū
incipit
¶Capl'm primū i collectōe intellect⁹
soc indicioz astrozū Proboemiū.

Erū M̄
J esure
i quib⁹
est pro
nostica
bil' scie
stellarū ū
profectō
magnas
τ pcipu
as duas
esse dep
hēdim⁹.
Quz altera quz pzecedit τ est soztioz.
et scientia Solis τ lune: nec nō. v. stel
larī eraticaz figuras demonstras: qs
toz motuū cā: τ mū⁹ ad aliā eozqz ad
vri collatione contingere manifestū
d̄. Altera vo est scia qua explanā τ mu
tiones τ opa:q̄ accidūt. τ cōpleni p̄
pz̄ figuras circuū cazz naturales eis
iēb⁹ quas circūdit. Sed q̄n dua pz̄
dicai:prima quidē est scientia per se
atoz icōmiza:opoz̄ts ut scie perscru
tat cam sui cā perquirat τ adiscat
be fuēci accipi at: lic̄ scōbam nō adi
ax scit. Qm ipī bic ita se bfe mani
testi est: τ ā p̄ez per se scie tibi a nobis

9 A horoscope from the earliest printed edition of Ptolemy's
Tetrabiblos, produced in Venice in 1482

9 An Arab astrologer, from a seventeenth-century Persian MS

10 St Augustine, by Sandro Botticelli

11 The fate of astrologers, as envisaged by Dante. Their heads are twisted to the rear as punishment for their attempts to look into the future

him with gifts and subsequently not only made him his confidant but also became his pupil.

The frequency with which incidents involving astrology
appear in Suetonius' *Lives* of the Caesars is a clear indication
of the increasing power and ubiquity of its grip on Roman
society. Nero was supposed to have executed a large number
of people, on the advice of his astrologer Balbillus, in order to
cancel the omens of a comet. Domitian was made to give an
unwitting demonstration of the truth of astrology. The astrologer Ascletarion had foolishly predicted Domitian's end and
was promptly condemned to death. Somewhat illogically,
Domitian then declared that he would show how nonsensical
astrological predictions were and demanded that Ascletarion
should predict how his own end would come. ' My body will
be torn to pieces by dogs ', he replied. Not so, the Emperor
retorted triumphantly and gave careful orders that the
astrologer should be burnt after execution and the ashes
scattered in the Tiber. Ascletarion was duly executed and the
executioners prepared to carry out the Emperor's orders,
placing the corpse upon a pyre and even getting as far as
lighting it. But a sudden storm not only sent them scurrying
for shelter but also put out the flames and a pack of the dogs of
Rome, fierce, semi-wild animals, seized the half-burnt corpse
and tore it to pieces before the executioners could prevent
them.

By the end of the first century AD astrology completely
dominated in Rome, achieving the status of a quasi-religion.
In AD 52 Claudius followed Augustus' lead and expelled
astrologers from the city. Unlike the first emperor, Claudius'
objection to the ' profession ' was intellectual, but he was no
more successful in suppressing it. The importation of the
mystery religions of the East resulted inevitably in the astrological renaissance. Even such a comparatively sober cult as
Mithraism, with its echoes and parallels to Christianity, would
necessarily encourage a more extravagant and fanciful interpretation of religion than the austerities of traditional Roman

religion. But as degeneration increased apace in Rome, achieving perhaps its ultimate in the extraordinary reign of Heliogabalus and his self-identification with the Sun-god, astrology seemed, if anything, an unexceptional and indeed sober occupation.

In the reign of Augustus a poet by the name of Manilius produced an immense rhymed treatise under the title of *Astronomics*. Apart from that one work, his name was to be unknown to posterity but the *Astronomics* presented, in a popular form, the doctrines which others had drawn from a number of obscure sources. Manilius summarised that ' correspondence ' between the human body and the tutelary star which, first enunciated by the so-called Hermes Trismegistus, was later to become the cornerstone of medicine.

The Ram, chief of the signs, has for his special province the head. The beauty of the human neck falls within the arbitrament of the bull. The two arms, with shoulders conjoined, are assigned in equal division to the Twins. The breast is placed under the Crab, the Lion holds sway over the sides and back. The loins come down to the Maid as her proper lot. The Balance governs the buttocks, the Scorpion has his glory in the genitals, the thighs are subject to the Centaur, Capricorn is lord of both the knees, the legs are the power of the Water-Carrier, and the Fishes claim for themselves the governance of the feet.

So widespread was the belief and practice of astrology that Petronius could tilt at it in his *Satyricon*, confident that his readers would recognise even recondite references. In the great banquet given by the Trimalchio, the dishes were chosen to represent the signs of the Zodiac while Trimalchio himself gave an impromptu lecture on their meaning, boasting that he was born under the Crab and so was well able to defend himself. Opposition to astrology was limited, but bitter and articulate. Cicero, although a personal friend of the astrologer Nigidius Figulus, mocked at the whole art and theory, posing the unanswerable objections that astrologers only too often blundered into some personal catastrophe which should have been clearly marked in their horoscopes and that twins, born within a few moments of each other and therefore subject to identical influences, should therefore have identical futures. Pliny pointed out that the planets were far too far away for their emanations to have the slightest effect upon human beings; Juvenal savagely attacked those who aped Oriental customs and religions – including astrology. Women came in for a particular merciless drubbing. Juvenal believing, or affecting to believe, that they consulted astrologers for the most sinister of reasons.

Chapter 4
The Challenge of Christianity

From the moment that astrology emerged from chaos into the possession of an accepted form and theory it impinged upon the world of religion. In some cultures it was tolerated, accepted as a byproduct of other, more vital activities and no more. In others it assumed a leading role, indistinguishable from the formal religious observances: Egyptian, Babylonian, Greek and Roman priests adopted this or that aspect of astrological theory and practice as it suited them. There could be no real distinction, between a religious concept which postulated a multiplicity of very anthropomorphic gods, and a philosophical view of the universe in which the wheeling planets and fixed stars affected a multiplicity of human fates second by second.

Christianity, while still struggling for its own form, was permeated with astrological theory. The Gnostics of the first century AD erected an elaborate *cultus* which retained the whirling crystalline spheres of Pythagoras, but changed their significance. The Gnostics viewed each of the spheres as a barrier between man and heaven, instead of being, at best, neutral and almost purely mathematical concepts. The soul, in descending to earth in preparation for birth in a human body, had to pass through each of these spheres and took from each some characteristic which dulled the pureness of its spiritual radiance. Each sphere was ruled by an Archon who attempted, after the person's death, to prevent his soul returning back to its source. The belief was, in part, an allegory of the Gnostic concept of the universe as being divided into two mutually exclusive elements, the purely spiritual and the purely material. The soul, before it could return to its source, had to shed every element of materialism – in short, had to pass through each of the seven spheres and divest itself of the characteristics it had borrowed on its journey to earth.

Such was the allegory which, imperceptibly, became changed into fact. The most dramatic evidence of this change was embodied in one of the Gnostic texts which spoke of the journey which Christ made through the spheres after his death and resurrection. Mary Magdalen asks him what will now be the role of the astrologers, seeing that he has passed through the spheres and disturbed their equilibrium. Christ replies:

> If the horoscope-casters find the Fate and the sphere turned towards the left, their words will come to pass, and they will say what is to take place. But if they chance on the Fate or the sphere turned to the right, they are bound to say nothing true.

The Gnostics recognised the power of the stars in human affairs even if they believed that power to be almost wholly malign. Such was the general belief of the early Christians. Christianity was busy turning the gods of Olympus into the devils of Hell, transforming cloven-footed Pan into Satan himself, and it was therefore logical that the theories and practices of astrology, being wholly pagan in their origins, should also be transformed into malevolent influences. Here and there were pockets of passive resistance, even as some of the attributes of the older gods persisted into the new world under the guise of witchcraft. Outstanding was the Star of Bethlehem, a purely astrological concept which survived into Christianity. In the *Clementine Recognitions*, it was held that, because Abraham had been an astrologer, he had been able to recognise his creator when other men had been blind.

The *Recognitions* were supposed to have been written by a certain Clement to James, the brother of Christ, and purported to be an account of the activities of the tiny band of Christians between the death and the Resurrection of Christ. They were, in fact, written sometime during the second century AD and provide a clear enough picture of the Christian view of astrology before the prestige of St Augustine banished the art from the canon in the fifth century. There was no question of the possibility of foretelling the future from the position of the stars at birth. The only problem was the ancient one of how to reconcile the apparently immutable future with the Christian doctrine of free will. The conflicting theories remained conflicting : the only way out for the good Christian was the hope that, with God's help, he could prove himself stronger than the stars.

In AD 313 the Edict of Milan gave freedom of worship to people of all religions within the Empire. In practice, the Edict was the establishment of Christianity which returned the compliment by seeking to extinguish all other religions within the Empire. Speculators such as the Gnostics became heretics and swiftly there developed a body of received opinion which was to be the orthodoxy of the future. By the end of the fourth century the ancient religions were in full retreat, proscribed as demonic organisations. And in retreat, too, was astrology.

It was St Augustine who led the attack upon it. In his youth he had in fact consulted astrologers and shared the common belief in the efficacy of the art they practised. But then, according to his *Confessions,* that belief was undermined on the day when he discovered that a certain very wealthy landowner had been born at the same moment as one of the slaves on his estate. It was a problem which astrologers had been avoiding for centuries but the implications remained lodged in Augustine's mind. He returned to it in one of his letters. Why was it, he wondered, that an astrologer could beat his wife, ' I won't say if he catches her being improperly playful, but even if she stares too long through a window ' ? Could not his wife retort that it was not her, but Venus who was at fault? The astrologer's whole art and profession, after all, was based on the assumption that human beings were moulded and controlled by forces outside their control.

But still Augustine had not pronounced the final condemnation of astrology. That came in his book *The City of God,* the work written after the traumatic experience of the sack of Rome in AD 410. Brooding over the whole problem of fate and God's will and human free will, he turned his attention to astrology. His attitude towards it was ambivalent : on the one hand he claimed that it was a fraud and a delusion, on the other that it usurped God's power over the universe, for if the movement of Jupiter or Venus could spell out some future event, this could only be by limiting the Creator's power to alter that future event. It was, admittedly, possible for astrologers accurately to predict some aspect of the future but this was done simply through the power of the Devil. The art of casting a horoscope itself was meaningless.

Augustine had spoken and for more than four centuries after that astrology was dismissed as a fool's goal. But it was never formally proscribed by the Church and a weak underground movement, led by scholars no means despicable, contrived to keep the art just discernibly alive in Europe. Firmicius Maternus made a determined attempt to reconcile astrology with Christianity in his book *Mathesis* – yet another attempt to create a synthesis of all knowledge. Synesius of Cyrene, who ended life as a bishop, looked on astrology as being the poor but honest handmaiden to theology itself. The universe was held together by sympathy, he wrote, a theory which was to be developed by C. G. Jung in the twentieth century.

The field of astrology is so wide and amorphous, touching at one extreme something which is almost indistinguishable from pure astronomy and, at the other, something which is quite indistinguishable from occult practices that, over the centuries, it has given shelter to men of astonishingly varied beliefs. A curiously impressive aspect of its survival has been its appearance in lands far distant from each other during periods when communications were limited to the painfully slow movement of pack-animals. Presumably, the common elements were due to a common origin and that common origin – again presumably – must be Mesopotamia. But the relative speed of transmission argues that the countries most distant from the common centre had developed or were groping towards a star-based philosophy upon which the aesthetically satisfying Babylonian system was merely imprinted. By about the first century AD places as far apart as China and India shared, with the Mediterranean countries, an astrological tradition whose correspondences were, to say the least, impressive. The fact that the planet, known to the West as Mars, should also be known to the East as a planet signifying war and disturbance generally might, perhaps, arise from its reddish colour. But why should Mercury – the planet assigned in the West to the fickle, thievish god of movement – be assigned similar qualities in the East? The goods that traders took with them from country to country tended to be of small bulk and of high intrinsic value. It seems unlikely that many would have given precious space to astrologers' manuscripts, and the complex arguments of astrological correspondence certainly could not have been transmitted by word of mouth. Rather remarkably, it would seem that peoples in parts of the world remote from each other, alien in language, customs and religions alike, unwittingly agreed to invest certain aspects of the heavens with very similar attributes. It is this casual correspondence which gives the sceptic pause, and creates defendants in the most unexpected places. There would appear to be a universal element in an art which has attracted, at different times, the attention of Pythagoras, a Greek philosopher, Aquinas, an Italian theologian, and Jung, a Swiss psychologist.

During the long decline of astrology in the West it was kept alive first in Alexandria and then in the Islamic countries. In Alexandria there developed the philosophy, later called Neoplatonism, which can be viewed either as the final flowering, or the ultimate collapse of the ancient philosophies. Essentially, it sought to combine the teachings of East and West, infusing Plato's philosophy with Oriental mysticism, and was to prove at once Christianity's great rival and the crucible for many of its concepts. The philosophy's major exponent was Plotinus, who was born in Egypt of Greek parents in AD 205 and later emigrated to Italy where he greatly influenced the emperor Gallienus and accordingly was granted the imperial protection during a chaotic period. Plotinus followed Plato in his conviction that man's end is to rise beyond earthly desires and reach communion with God, but his philosophy was essentially pantheistic regarding the manifestations of the physical world as direct emanations from God. Astrology with its claim to be unifying, naturally attracted his attention. The stars, he argued, could virtually be regarded as gods in their own right, but despite their beauty and power they moved within an all-embracing framework. Vigorously he refuted the argument that they controlled fate: stars and men alike were only elements in creation and while the movement and pattern of the stars could be used to trace out the course of future events, they no more controlled those events than a map controlled the physical features of the terrain it represented.

In Europe, astrology went into a decline for over five hundred years. There was no overt attack upon it, nor were its practitioners fearful of being mistaken for witches and burnt for their activities. In part, the long eclipse arose from the Christian rejection of pagan philosophy: astrology was born of heathenism, and was part and parcel of a now despised cult. In part, the bent of man's minds seems to have changed: the teachers and the philosophers and the leaders of society were dedicated to a more austere search than their predecessors. Not for them was magic, or synthesis or correspondence a royal path to truth : instead they favoured a rigorous exercise of pure intellect – although, paradoxically, astrology would return to Europe in the baggage of the medieval ' Schoolmen ' who, above all, chopped logic for a living. As a result of its neglect by serious minds, it fell into more and ever more dubious hands, becoming at last indistinguishable from the grossest of peasant superstitions.

But across the Mediterranean, in the Arab world, astrology was kept alive with some of its former dignity and sense of purpose. In Harun al-Raschid's fabulous city of Baghdad a great observatory arose, much as the ziggurats had risen, in the same land, to undertake a study that was as much astronomical as astrological. It was here that the great Albumasar conducted his studies, under the protection of the caliph, in the ninth century. His book on astrology, the *Introductiorum in Astronomiam*, was probably the very first work on the subject to be printed after the invention of the printing press and was destined to have an enormous influence on Renaissance astrologers. Much of it was devoted to the grammar of astrology. It was this aspect, indeed, which first ensured its survival and then its popularity, for those who paid out good gold to have it copied were initially interested only in the technical information it preserved and transmitted from antiquity. But Albumasar also grappled with the problems which had presented themselves to the Neoplatonists – the ancient problems of free will and the degree of control exercised by the heavenly bodies. He made a distinction between the influence of the planets and of the fixed stars : the former controlled – or could control – the details of everyday life : the latter affected only the grand design of the universe itself in a manner so slowly, and on such an enormous scale, as to be scarcely visible to the human eye and barely affecting human destiny at all. And free will? Albumasar wriggled out of the problem with a dexterity which would have aroused the admiration of the most finicky logic-chopper in the West. There are two kinds of actions – necessary and

12 Christian view of Arabian astrologers 1513

contingent: necessary actions were produced by certain conditions: contingent actions were produced by changeable causes. Exactly what kind of action was produced by what kind of cause seems to have been largely the decision of the astrologer, a fact which would give him very wide leeway in the interpretation of his client's chart – and excellent excuses afterwards.

By the end of the tenth century the Baghdad caliphate was in eclipse, but Arabic culture was to find an outlet in a totally unexpected place at the other end of the Mediterranean. For centuries, Arab and Christian were to live shoulder by shoulder in the Iberian peninsula, again and again exhorted to go on holy war against each other, sometimes actually doing so but, nevertheless, inescapably influencing each other. And it was from Spain, Islam's bridgehead in Europe, that the ancient cult of astrology was to make its way again into Europe and find distinguished patrons. It was in Spain that the future Pope Sylvester was educated and there learned those arts which, at the turn of the millennium, in Rome, were to earn him the name of magician. He converted one of the towers of the Lateran Palace into an observatory and, inevitably, was suspected of having dealings with the Devil.

Sylvester was interested only in ' pure ' astronomy and it was largely through him that the Pythagorean concept of the Seven Spheres began to edge out of the cruder concept of the limited and flat earth. But astronomy's ' foolish daughter ' astrology also enjoyed a renaissance. Robert Grosseteste, the first known Chancellor of Oxford University, roundly stated that astrology not merely allowed man to peer into the future but actually controlled every aspect of life on earth. On the Continent the great Dominican Albertus Magnus held a belief just as extreme. And Albertus Magnus had for pupil no less a person than the Angelic Doctor himself – Thomas Aquinas.

The fact that the master had embraced astrology did not necessarily imply that the pupil would obediently do the same – particularly considering that the pupil was Thomas Aquinas.

But Aquinas was predisposed to accept that the stars had some effect on human destiny because the belief had been worked into the teachings of Aristotle, who had himself been influenced by Pythagoras. By the early Middle Ages Aristotle had a position in the Christian universe that would have astonished him – and doubtless many an early Christian who would have dismissed him as an outrider of Satan. The Aristotelian universe, with its interlocking causes and, ultimately, its first cause, neatly fitted both the intangible world of Christian morality and the mechanical world of the astrologers. Aquinas took over part of the teachings of his master, Albertus Magnus, in this matter. The stars were, for him, something between an agent and a principal: they were one of the channels of the Creator's will – the means whereby he controlled the actual physical bodies of men. This, neatly enough, left room for the operation of free will for while many men were, in fact, controlled by their bodies – i.e. their lusts for material things – and were hence under the direct influence of the stars – it was perfectly possible for them to make themselves the master.

And with this blessing from Christianity's supreme logician, astrology emerged at last from its dusty ignoble hiding places to stand beside theology and astronomy and geometry, dominating learning and influencing the pattern of social life for nearly five centuries.

E

Chapter 5
Astrologers of the Renaissance

In the closing years of the thirteenth century the city of Forli in Central Italy was afflicted by the same insensate partisan warfare between Guelfs and Ghibellines which was tearing apart the majority of other Italian cities. At various periods, and under greater or lesser pressure, a truce would be patched up between the heads of the factions but, inevitably, it would be broken and the city plunged once again into bloodshed and confusion.

Guido Bonatto – scholar, astronomer and official astrologer to the city fathers – undertook to repair the breach once and for all. After much impressive study he announced to his fellow citizens that this could be achieved provided that they followed his precise instructions. The walls of the city – which were, in any case, in need of repair – were to be rebuilt under a constellation to be chosen by himself. Two citizens, one Guelf and the other Ghibelline, were each to cement a foundation stone at the precise moment when the constellation rose.

All went forward smoothly until the auspicious moment. The entire population of Forli – some 50,000 men, women and children – were assembled to witness the miracle. The two selected men were solemnly given their foundation stones, supplied with trowels and mortar, and waited. Bonatto, who was an astronomer of no mean skill, kept his eyes fixed upon

13   Guido Bonatto, leader of the astrological revival in thirteenth century Italy

his instrument with his right hand held high above his head.
At the exact moment he called out triumphantly 'Now' and
brought his hand down with a crash upon the table. The
Ghibelline obediently dropped his stone into position and
industriously began to cement it into place. The other man
hesitated and then, with the eyes of all his fellow citizens upon
him, he threw his stone to the ground. Bonatto, he declared,
was a crypto-Ghibelline and the whole ceremony had been
devised to harm the Guelf party. 'God damn thee and the

whole Guelf party with your distrustful malign', Bonatto cried. 'This constellation will not appear above our city again for another 500 years.'

The abortive reconciliation in Forli could not have been better designed to illustrate the extraordinary hold which astrology again exerted upon a vigorous, intelligent and essentially practical people after centuries in decline and obscurity. It reappeared first in Italy, partly, perhaps, as a result of the religious scepticism which was at work in the early thirteenth century and later as a byproduct of the passionate interest in antiquity. And if any one man were to be held responsible for that revival, whether in praise or blame, that man would be Guido Bonatto himself. As with all these earlier practitioners, it is impossible to divorce the charlatan – if he existed – from the scholar, the artist from the scientist, the astronomer from the astrologer. Later, when his great book, the *Liber Astronomicus,* could be compared with the works of such men as Copernicus or Kepler it could be seen for what it was, an ill-digested farrago of Greek and Arab learning, heavily spiced with pure mythology and his own idiosyncratic interpretations of the classic astrological systems. But the book must have possessed some spark of originality, for it became, and remained, immensely popular both with the laity and with working astrologers, long after pure science had shown it up for the sorry farce that it was. As late as 1676 the English astrologer William Lilly translated it and introduced it into England – ten years after Isaac Newton had begun to consider the motion of the moon.

Bonatto was taken into the entourage of the most feared and hated man of his day, the condottiero Ezzelino da Romano, sharing the office with a Saracen, Paul of Baghdad. Some believed that Ezzelino's appalling excesses of cruelty could be directly attributed to his astrologers on the grounds that he was merely attempting to forestall this or that evil confidently predicted for him. But his patron's ill-fame by no means adversely affected Bonatto's career. After Ezzelino had

14 The signs and professions controlled by Jupiter. The professions are, from left to right, an apothecary, an alchemist and a moneylender

15 Part of the fresco, illustrating the months of the year, painted by Francesco del Cossa for the Duke of Ferrara. March is represented by the figure of a girl (Spring) over Aries the Ram

16 Another part of the fresco depicting April (a youth holding the key of Spring) seated above Taurus. The fresco was designed by the court astrologer

been cut down – dying like an animal, ripping off the bandages that his enemies had placed on his wounds – the Saracen disappeared but Bonatto, like some parasite abandoning the dead body of its host, nimbly joined the nomadic court of another war-lord, Guido da Montefeltro. Notwithstanding the fact that Bonatto had somehow overlooked the manner in which his late employer would come to an end, Montefeltro reposed the fullest confidence in him. Bonatto's task was to approve the object of each marauding expedition and choose the hour for setting forth. So besotted was Montefeltro with his astrologer that he even allowed him to control the moment of departure like a military exercise: Bonatto would strike a bell to signify the moment for donning armour, a second to order the men to horseback and the third to start the march.

Bonatto's reputation with Montefeltro survived even his disastrous meteorological duel with a peasant. As the story went the rounds, Montefeltro was taking the air in the main square of Forli when a peasant came up and gave him a basket of fruit. Touched, the great soldier invited the man to dinner but he refused on the grounds that it was going to rain. Montefeltro summoned Bonatto who pooh-poohed the idea: he could hardly do otherwise, having predicted fine weather. Obstinately the peasant declared that there would be a very heavy shower, basing his prediction on the restlessness of his donkey. He declined to take Bonatto's assurance, departed ' and an hour afterwards lo! it began to thunder and there was a great downpouring of waters. Then Guido began to cry out with indignation " Who has deluded me? Who has put me to shame?" And for a long time this was a great source of merriment among the people.'

Montefeltro, smitten by religious doubts, ended his career in a monastery. Bonatto, despite the unsavoury nature of his employers, despite the mockery that attended him whenever ' rain ' was mentioned, easily found new employment. And not the least extraordinary part of his remarkable career was the fact that his third patron was no credulous warrior with a strong arm and a thick head but the Republic of Florence, a city accustomed to weigh everything in the scales of commercial profit. His salary was paid in the hard-earned gold of sober merchants: his appointment had to be approved by professional civil servants jealously guarding their own prerogatives – Guido Bonatto could fairly claim to have arrived and to have made a respectable profession out of an activity that once might have earned him the stake. Not all the Florentines approved. The great Dante sourly thrust him into hell, placing him among that group of people who are condemned to go through eternity with their heads twisted to the rear as punishment for trying to look ahead.

Bonatto failed in one rather important matter: he did not predict his own death at the hands of robbers not far from his native city. Significantly, he was returning from a tour of lectures he had given in French and Italian universities, for the astrologer was now an honoured professional, sharing the lecture dais with the astronomer and the physician and, as often as not, combining all three roles. Apologists for Bonatto's trade argued that there would have been little point in his predicting his own death, for there was nothing he could have done to avoid it. Pierleoni of Spoleto provided the bleak, pragmatic answer to those who claimed that, somehow, free will continued to operate within the framework of the stars. He foresaw his own death by water and in consequence took every possible means to avoid water, even turning down lucrative appointments in Venice and Padua because the threshold of chance was raised a little too high. He did in fact die by drowning – and by suicide – for being charged of complicity in a plot he threw himself into the river. His was the classic example of a man virtually willing himself to death. He had predicted that he would die by water: the thought had haunted him for years so that when at last he was subjected to great stress the way of release was only too obvious.

'Vir sapiens dominabitur astris' – the wise man is master of the stars – so men proclaimed hopefully. But it is significant that the apothegm should be in use at all, arguing as it does that men had the gravest doubts on that subject. The astrologer with his instruments and charts was present at every state function, every private occasion of sufficient importance to warrant the expense of his presence. The Church, which had once robustly dismissed the whole apparatus of fortune-telling under the forthright phrase of ' charms, omens, dreams and such-like foolishness ', now gave the highest support to astrology. The tough, eminently practical politician Pope Julius II had the day for his coronation chosen by an astrologer and later declined to leave Bologna for Rome until his court astrologer had picked an auspicious day. The courtly Leo X, the Maecenas of the sixteenth century, prided himself not only on the fact that the arts were flourishing as never before in his pontificate but that astrology, too, was honoured and practised. The cardinals of Paul III were faced with the delicate problem of deciding Christian affairs in terms of a pagan art, for their master declined to hold a Consistory until an exact hour had been chosen astrologically.

The day for a coronation, the hour for a Consistory – this was admittedly unimportant, not affecting the matter under discussion by any significant degree. But it was when the astrologer became involved in political and military decisions that posterity finds itself almost wholly at a loss to account for his role in society. In a war between Pisa and Florence, the Florentines commissioned their official astrologer to fix an auspicious hour for the departure of reinforcements – and nearly lost a vital battle because the astrologer insisted that the army take a certain circuitous route out of the city so that it arrived hours later than it should. Nevertheless, these same level-headed Florentine businessmen – who would have exiled or even executed a general for making such a decision – calmly continued to allow their astrologer to make vital decisions for them on no other authority than his familiarity with the distant stars.

An extreme example of this curious dichotomy in government was provided by the first Visconti duke of Milan. Visconti was, for all practical purposes, the equivalent of the twentieth century tycoon. He had no interest in glory, little interest in art and seems to have been totally immune from any religious doubts or beliefs. His sole passion lay in the technique of government and its ancillary activities of finance and war, ever preferring to use bribery to force. Working like an unobtrusive mole, planning years and indeed decades ahead, he created an immense and powerful state out of a number of fragments. Nevertheless, this essentially practical politician, whom all other Italians simultaneously admired and feared for his cold grasp of essentials, habitually employed two astrologers. One of them, Gusperto da Maltraversi, was his personal physician and was a man of considerable skill in his legitimate profession but he enjoyed far more fame practising his occult works. It is difficult to see how Visconti could reconcile his own deeply experienced knowledge of the measures which had to be taken for a particular political goal and the possibly contradictory advice of his non-political astrologer. Presumably, if Maltraversi were misguided enough to give a too-divergent opinion, the prince's own common sense would override the astrological dictum. The probability is that. Maltraversi himself was very well aware of what his employer would do under a given circumstance and therefore took care that the horoscope matched the circumstance. It was, in addition, a standard practice to read backwards from an event. Visconti had himself achieved supreme power in the state by overthrowing his uncle. It was undoubtedly Maltraversi who later announced that Jupiter, Saturn and Mars stood in the house of the Twins at the time – a highly auspicious conjunction. Equally doubtless, however, Maltraversi had not been party to the well-kept secret of the conspiracy and could therefore only have cast the horoscope for it after it had happened. There seems little more point in doing this than in reconstructing a game of chess after its conclusion. The interest is purely academic but it would give the ' native ' – the person for whom the horoscope is cast – a pleasant feeling of having his action approved by the gods.

One of the odder aspects of the Renaissance is that this period which exalted reason and the human intellect even above religion, should also have given birth to three extraordinary systems, belief in which required an almost total suspension of common sense. The rise of witchcraft, alchemy and of astrology all took place much about the same period. All three had been present in European culture for centuries but in a subordinate, literally occult manner. Now, suddenly, it seemed as though the night sky were crowded with witches hastening to the Sabbath, alchemists were to be found at every street corner and, with them, the astrologer. It would be difficult to make any final distinction between witch, alchemist and astrologer. In the popular mind, indeed, they were frequently seen as one and the same person, the powers of each overlapping. The witch was very largely a figment of judicial imagination but the alchemist was a very real person pursuing an arduous and honourable profession. In his endless search for the Philosopher's Stone, a search during which he examined every metal, every substance which could be chemically changed by heat, it was natural that he should turn to the great sister art of astrology which claimed, in its turn, to control or influence every element in creation.

Even at the height of his influence, the alchemist tended to be looked at askance – probably because everybody had at least one story to tell of a charlatan who had made gold for himself if not for his client. But astrology now was supported by the most brilliant, the most influential figures. Martin Luther noted gravely: ' The signs in heaven and earth are surely not lacking: they are God's and the angels' work, and they warn and threaten the godless lands and countries and have significance.' That ebullient extrovert Philippus Theophrastus Bombastus von Hohenheim, who called himself Paracelsus and infuriated his medical colleagues by performing miracle cures, swept astrology into his compendious system –

and anticipated psychiatry in doing so. The major virtue in employing astrology in medicine, he declared, was in order to unlock the secrets festering in the human heart. The mathematician Johann Müller, who called himself Regiomontanus, was no theoretical astronomer but an observational one, a

17 The fraudulent astrologer receives a client

man, moreover, with the skill and imagination to invent his own instruments. But, purely practical though his work was, it was he who tackled the impossible problem of astrological ' houses ' – the twelve divisions of the sky through which the planets march – and created a system which, for all its manifest weaknesses, has never since been bettered by astrologers.

The astrologer now could command handsome fees if his equipment were elaborate enough, his tongue glib enough and his forecasts supple enough. Most universities had a chair in astrology and wealthy families, while they might not maintain their own astrologers, certainly paid a retainer to the most successful one in the city. ' In all the better families the horoscope of the children was drawn up as a matter of course, and it sometimes happened that for half a lifetime men were haunted by the idle expectation of events which never occurred ', Jacob Burckhardt noted. In his great work on the Italian Renaissance, Burckhardt gave a key place to astrology as one of the modifying factors at work in society. ' The stars were questioned whenever a great man had to come to any important decision, and even consulted as to the hour at which any undertaking was to be begun. The journeys of princes, the reception of foreign ambassadors, the laying of the foundation stone of public building depend on the answer.' The emblems found their way again and again into art, culminating in that beautiful series of Frescoes which Francesco del Cossa executed for the Duke of Ferrara. A complex series of correspondences were worked out connecting the planets with the rise and fall of religions – a concept which could have done nothing but contribute to the essential scepticism of the period. Thus it was argued that the conjunction of Jupiter with Saturn had brought the faith of Israel into existence : Jupiter with Mars had produced the Chaldean : with the Sun, the religion of ancient Egypt : with Venus the Mohammedan. Christianity had been brought about through the conjunction of Jupiter with Mercury – and would end when Jupiter conjoined with the Moon for this, in turn, would bring the reign of Antichrist.

At the beginning of the revival of astrology in Italy a certain Checco d'Ascoli had been burnt at the stake for casting Christ's horoscope and thereby deducing the inevitability of the crucifixion. Now astrologers could openly argue that the religion of Christ had been brought into being by the wheeling motion of the planets, which would also bring it to an end. Implicit belief was held in the wildest assertions of the astrologers. Indeed, it seemed that the wilder, the more improbable the assertion, the more abject and uncontradicted was that belief. In 1524 Italy, along with all Europe, was waiting for the appalling flood which had been predicted a quarter of a century earlier. A German, Johannes Stoffler, had discovered that all seven planets would be in conjunction in the watery sign of Pisces – an infallible indication that the known world must be destroyed by water. Over those twenty-five years, astrologers had returned again and again to the problem like a dog worrying at a bone. Each examination, each re-casting only proved Stoffler's terrible prediction. Some few fundamentalists argued that this could not possibly be true for had not God set the rainbow in the sky as promise that never again would the floodgates of heaven be opened? Few shared the comfortable belief and as the fatal year approached, pamphlets poured from the newborn press, warning, advising, giving what comfort there was to be had. Shipbuilders made immense profits as those who could afford it chartered every available craft in the ports. Those who lived inland even built their own version of the Ark. And waited. The world escaped yet again – unless the deluge perhaps occurred in Australia or the Americas : the quicker-thinking astrologers congratulated Christianity for the strength of its prayers in turning aside the calamity while others perhaps looked for another profession. But while there was a few weeks of embarrassment for the astrologers of Europe, the whole incident had been forgotten within a month or so and astrologers were again accepting invitations to cast the horoscope of this infant prince or that republic.

Nevertheless, the cult, all-pervading though it was, could not wholly occlude the luminous Latin intellect. In the earlier period Francesco Petrarch, the great scholar and poet, had added astrologers to the list of people he hated most. In his clear and vivid prose he described their tricks as precisely and as accurately as though he himself were a reformed astrologer. He had a particular and personal reason to dislike astrologers. In 1350 he had been given the honour of pronouncing the formal oration at the installation of the new Lord of Milan, and as was his custom, he laboured greatly to produce a perfect Latin speech. He was halfway through it when the official astrologer whose task it was to announce the exact moment when the new regime started, attempted to interrupt him. Before the shocked gaze of the assembled thousands of Milanese citizens the two took part in an undignified wrangle, no less bitter because it was conducted in an undertone. The astrologer, inevitably, won : no matter how much the Lord of Milan might esteem Petrarch's scholarship, he was taking no chances on commencing his reign at an inauspicious moment. Francesco Petrarch was left with the mangled remnants of his speech.

But the great enemy of astrology in the sixteenth century was the humanist scholar Pico della Mirandola. His hatred seems to have arisen from two separate causes : as a scholar he objected to the dubious logic of the system and as a Christian he objected even more to the fatalism inherent in it. If the planets really controlled human destiny, he argued, then they must obviously be superior to God – and therefore should be worshipped in the place of the Creator. He went to endless trouble to amass evidence against astrologists.

I have been taking note of weather conditions for a whole winter and checking them against predictions. On the 130 days or more that I made my observations, there were only six or seven which agreed with the published predictions.

Making sport of meteorologists is a time-honoured occupation : in 1947 British newspapers ran an hilarious scoreboard in which a Cornish farmer's predictions based on the activities of gnats were, for some weeks, far more accurate for his area than were the official bulletins. But Pico della Mirandola had, in addition, his immense prestige. Scholarship in Renaissance Italy was a tightknit, almost family affair with everybody knowing what everybody else was doing and thinking. Pico's reasoned, sustained onslaught upon the astrologers and their creed had a rapid success. Crude fortunetellers still continued to ply their trade in the market place, extracting coppers from peasants in return for highly coloured predictions of the stars. But the astrologer was virtually kicked out of the court. One of the most dramatic indications of the changed status of astrology was provided by Raphael in his decorations for the cupola of the Chigi palace. There, the planets and constellations were shown as conventional gods – but each was under the control of an angel and all clearly subservient to the Creator.

Nevertheless, so firmly was astrology rooted in European culture, so clearly did it respond to some deepseated need of the human psyche that even the shattering astronomical discoveries of Copernicus, Kepler and Galileo failed to make little if any difference to the popular mind. At the beginning of the fifteenth century there were two clear, conflicting views regarding the universe. The orthodox view held by the Church and the universities was based on Aristotle and Ptolemy and claimed that it was the earth that was at the centre of the universe with the sun and other planets obediently marching around her. The Pythagorean concept of crystalline spheres swinging around the sun was logically attractive but held by only a few. Copernicus was an analytical, more than an observational, astronomer: it was by comparing the scores of existing astronomical theories based on the two great concepts that he at last came down in favour of the Pythagorean. For nearly thirty years he kept his researches private, not so much from fear of persecution – he was, in fact, in high favour with the Church – as from a wholesome fear of ridicule, the heliocentric universe was so utterly at odds with the common-sense view. It was in vain that he argued from classical literature: ' It is the same thing as Aeneas says in Virgil, " We sail forth from the harbour, and lands and cities retire ".' The ordinary man knew better when he could actually *see* the sun going round the earth.

Copernicus' discoveries had no effect on astrology. There

was no reason why they should, for it left the position of the planets unaltered relative to the Earth and solar influence was unaffected by the fact that it emanated from a fixed and not a moving source. Copernicus, indeed, may very well have maintained a belief in astrology and certainly his epochal book *On the Revolution of Celestial Orbs* was promptly pressed into the service of astrological prediction.

It was Tycho Brahe who, ironically, dealt a heavy blow both to astrology and to the Aristotelian cosmology on which astrologists had worked for more than a millenary and a half. Ironically, because Brahe rejected Copernicus' heliocentric universe and was, in fact, a practising astrologer. In 1572 he predicted that the comet which had appeared that year would have its greatest influence in 1592 when there would be a male child born in Finland destined for great things as a man, and that this man would die in 1632 in a religious battle. It might have been a lucky shot: in 1594 Gustavus Adolphus was born in Sweden and was killed at the battle of Lutzen in 1632.

But it was this same comet of 1572 which shattered the carefully constructed, delicately balanced universe of astrology. Brahe proved conclusively that the comet, in fact, emanated from a nova – an exploding star in the constellation of Cassiopeia. Astrologers had at first welcomed this flaring light in the sky, using it as basis for an impressive variety of predictions ranging from the end of the world to the birth of a new Messiah. Their euphoria was shortlived: Brahe's discovery had shattered for ever the concept of the eternally fixed stars in the 'eighth sphere'. The patterns of the constellations were not immutable but as fluid as any other object in nature. Even as religion was forced to re-think a large number of premises based on the concept of a fixed and central earth, so astrologers would be forced to refashion that neatly packaged heaven so clearly demonstrated by Ptolemy and his hundreds of followers.

Brahe produced an enormous quantity of observational

data during his lifetime – data whose significance he probably did not fully appreciate but which, in the hands of his assistant Johann Kepler, was to lay the foundations of modern astronomy. It was Kepler who coined the phrase of astrology being the 'foolish daughter' of astronomy – but the full context of the phrase throws some light on his ambiguous beliefs and personality. 'Astronomy, the wise mother: astrology, the foolish little daughter selling herself to any and every client willing and able to pay so as to maintain her wise mother alive.' Bereft of its poetical double meanings the statement has only one meaning: Johann Kepler, the first of the modern astronomers, either believed in astrology – or was prepared to exploit the belief of others in order to pay for his astronomical researches. The fact that he published astrological calendars was of comparatively little significance for they were only a few degrees removed from practical astronomical tables. But he actively entered the field of prediction, forecasting, among other political events, the Austrian retreat from the Turks in 1595. He cast the horoscope of the German general Wallenstein in 1608 – but somehow overlooked the fact that Wallenstein was going to be assassinated, although – to be fair – he did predict that the year 1634 would be a year of disorders and it was at this time that Wallenstein was murdered. Altogether, the strong probability is that Johann Kepler used his position at the imperial court to pick up political information and employed no other skill in predicting than that used by an intelligent man extrapolating from known facts and tendencies to the unknown.

Outside politics, he undoubtedly went back to a Pythagorean concept of the role that the stars played in religion. He held a complex belief that the rays from the stars, in striking the earth at different angles, sounded different notes, the whole blending into one harmonious chord. This was an obvious echo of the Pythagorean 'music of the spheres' but he took the matter a step further by arguing that, if anything, it was man who affected the stars rather than vice versa. The analogy he used was that of music: without man's hearing music would be non-existent or meaningless. Similarly, the only evil in the heavens was that projected by man himself.

In 1609 Galileo Galilei learned that 'a certain Fleming had constructed a spyglass by means of which visible objects, though very distant from the eyes of the observer, were distinctly seen as though nearby'. Intrigued, Galileo investigated further and within a year had perfected the instrument which would be known as the telescope. Almost immediately, he threw the world of astrology into a dizzy spin with his discovery of four satellites of Jupiter. How did they fit into the traditional cosmology of seven planets? What influences could they be deemed to exert? There was not then, nor could there ever be, any final answer but it pointed up for astrologers the fact that their tidy, interlocking universe had gone for ever. Henceforth, the astrologer would have to be as intellectually supple as the scientist or theologian, ever prepared to slip new facts into an ever-changing picture. Galileo himself provided an ironical comment on that old safe world that was gone for ever. In 1609 he drew up the horoscope of the Grand Duke of Tuscany, promising his client many years of active, profitable life. The Grand Duke disobligingly died a few weeks later.

F

Chapter 6

Astrology in England

Astrology had followed a path in England that was the very opposite to that which it had followed in Italy, for it began in scepticism and ended in a flood of almanacs. Before the sixteenth century, astrological references in literature are few and far between. The most outstanding was Chaucer – and he was almost wholly hostile to the concept. He could describe the Wife of Bath in light-hearted astrological terms –

> Venus me yaf my lust, my likerousnesses
> And Mars yaf me my sturdy hardyness –

but the astrologers themselves were dismissed as charlatans every ready to batten on fools.

'How happy are astrologers who are believed if they tell one truth to a hundred lies, while other people lose all credit if they tell one lie to a hundred truths', Francesco Guicciardini had noted ironically in Italy. Two hundred years after Chaucer, Shakespeare took up a similar theme. Edmund, in *King Lear*, mocks the common belief. 'This is the excellent foppery of the world, that when we are sick in fortune – often the surfeit of our own behaviour – we make guilty of our disasters the sun, the moon, the stars', and Cassius takes the point up again in *Julius Caesar*: 'Men at some time are masters of their fates. The fault, dear Brutus, is not in our stars, but in ourselves.' But while England's premier poet was echoing the Catholic Church's contempt of fortune tellers and astrologers, England's monarch was attempting to guide the state with at least half an ear open to the advice, warnings and exhortations of ' hyr astrologer ', Dr John Dee.

Dee harks back to an older, darker ancestry than do most of the Renaissance astrologers. The majority of his colleagues, whether in England or on the Continent, paid at least lip service to the new sciences. Dee was by no means ignorant of the changed direction of learning. He was, after all, a personal friend of Gerald Mercator and had begun his professional career as a mathematician. But whether through chance, or intellectual conviction, he went deeper and deeper into the pseudo-science of necromancy, earning a peculiarly unpleasing reputation as he became involved with the notorious Edward Kelly – although which of them was using the other it is impossible to say.

John Dee was born in 1527, studied mathematics and astronomy at Cambridge and, after travelling abroad to visit outstanding mathematicians – including Mercator – he took his MA in 1548. In the same year, however, he had to leave England in a hurry on suspicion of being a conjurer, a term indistinguishable from that of ' warlock '. His crime had been to produce a too-clever piece of stage machinery in which a giant beetle seemed actually to fly, carrying a man on its back. The scant, if awe-struck, descriptions make it difficult to decide whether the effect was made mechanically or, rather more likely, optically.

On his return to England three years later he was granted a pension by the young King Edward, which he later exchanged for the rectory of Upton-upon-Severn. The grant demonstrated, if nothing else, the somewhat amorphous nature of English Christianity at the period, for Dee was already well known as an astrologer and, according to others, as a witch. On the accession of Mary he found himself in prison, charged with using enchantments against the Queen's life. The charge probably arose out of a prophecy he was supposed to have made on news of the Queen's projected Spanish marriage:

> Woe to the two nations: Woe and sorrow
> Disaster by water: persecution by fire
> And the queen shall childless die.

It also seems that he was incautious enough to predict Elizabeth's accession to the throne. Nothing could be proved against him, and after languishing for some months in prison he was freed by order of the Privy Council. The incident was to stand him in good stead, however. The young Elizabeth, hungry for any sign of encouragement in her desperate state, remembered his optimistic prophecies and the moment she learned that she had, indeed, succeeded to the throne she summoned Dee to her and commissioned him to choose an auspicious day for the coronation.

Poor Dee must have felt that, after years of obscurity and frustration, he had at last come into the success that he deserved, for Elizabeth, in her expansive manner, made him the largest promises. He was, in fact, to occupy an important position at court, but little material benefit came his way, for Elizabeth was as cannily vague in fulfilling promises as she was prodigal in making them. Some of his activities were straightforward matters of state, such as his investigations into the Queen's title to land recently discovered by her subjects, or legal investigations which he substantiated with valuable geographical descriptions. He turned his attention, too, to the perennial problem of reform of the calendar. But it was his occult activities which fascinated the Queen and kept her interest in him alive. When a wax image of her was found, in Lincoln's Inn Fields, with a pin stuck in its breast, it was Dee who was instructed to investigate the matter. He came to the conclusion that it was merely a practical joke. He did not disclose the grounds on which he made such a decision, apparently flying in the face of the ominous evidence, and it speaks much for his influence with the Queen – mortally afraid as she was of death – that she simply accepted his word.

18 Dr John Dee,
Astrologer to Queen
Elizabeth I

19 William Lilly

20 Ebenezer Silbey, within his own horoscope

The guidance of the stars was naturally sought in the perilous days of the Armada and here it seems that Dee came into conflict with the Fleet captains. The sailing of a fleet had its own mystique of wind and tide : it mattered little whether an army marched out at one hour rather than another but such a margin of time could be fatal for a ship. But Elizabeth insisted that her sea-captains should listen to her astrologer. The probability is that the information which Dee provided was as much meteorological as astrological and may very well have shaped the overall naval strategy. Some of Dee's apologists go even further and claim that it was his opposition which prevented Drake from attacking the Armada before it actually left the Spanish ports of assembly. But it is doubtful if even Elizabeth would have gone quite so far and it is far more likely that Dee discreetly tailored his prediction and advice to reflect Elizabeth's own predilections.

During the greater part of his career Dee's major interest, outside his legitimate scholastic interests, was in astrology. It was in 1581, when he was over fifty, that he first came into contact with Edward Kelly and his life thereafter became intertwined with this enigmatic man. Kelly's own profession was that of apothecary, but that sank progressively further into the background as he developed the far more profitable trade of alchemist. He claimed to have discovered that Philosopher's Stone which was the goal of all alchemists, the key to all wealth and wisdom. Certainly, whatever it was that he had actually found brought him a thin trickle of gold from the purses of the credulous but his ambition went higher than that and it was a fortunate moment for him when he came into contact with the famous Dr Dee, mathematician extraordinary and astrologer to her Majesty.

It is difficult to see what the initial attraction was for Dee himself. In his diary, he noted that his first successful attempt at crystal-gazing occurred shortly after he met Kelly. How far Dee was deluding himself, and how far he possessed some paranormal faculty it is now impossible to determine. But he, certainly, seemed to link his psychic powers with Kelly.

Edward Kelly was undoubtedly a con-man of some ability. He was a charlatan and a rogue – his cropped ears bore official witness to that fact. John Dee was something of an innocent, the natural prey for such a man as Kelly. But it seems possible that the two men sparked off in each other some faculty which would not otherwise have existed. It was rather as if, together, they created a third personality which dissolved when they were apart.

Dee took up the hunt for the philosophers' stone on his own account, presumably not wholly convinced in the reality of the one which his colleague claimed to possess. Together, the two embarked on pure necromancy, conjuring up the angels Uriel and Michael to act as guide. Again, Dee probably deluded himself as to the reality of these entities – but he was able to describe the execution of Mary, Queen of Scots some four years before the event, in a vision supposedly given him by Uriel. His home at Mortlake in Surrey became the goal alternatively of those who sought prevision into the future, and those who wished to burn either Dr Dee or his many books on the reasonable suspicion of communicating with the Devil.

Life in Surrey seems to have become rather too hot for him, for he accepted, with Kelly, a Polish nobleman's invitation to return with him to his native country. They remained abroad for over eight years, travelling between Bohemia and Poland, living now in luxury, now in abject squalor depending upon the scepticism or the credulity of those whom they entertained. For it was as common mountebanks that Edward Kelly and Dr John Dee earned their living during those precarious years until at last they quarrelled and separated. The remarkable thing about their relationship is that it endured for as long as it did, for they were an ill-assorted couple. Dee was, at least, a scholar in origins and at heart and John Aubrey described him as an extremely handsome and aristocratic-looking man – tall, slender, with a curiously delicate complexion and the later dignity of a long white beard, contrasting unfavourably with the squat, cropeared Kelly.

Nevertheless, Kelly had provided the dynamic in their relationship, for after Dee returned to England in 1594 he dabbled no more in spiritualism or alchemy. He was an old man now – approaching his seventies although in splendid health – and, despite his somewhat murky past, was honoured successively with the chancellorship of St Paul's Cathedral and the wardenship of Manchester College, evidence that the scholar had not wholly disappeared under the necromancer. But he was to endure once more the petty disappointments which had studded his career and whose accumulation had held him from the high office he might have enjoyed. He had gained little enough materially from the confidence which Elizabeth placed in him – but even that little he lost when the pedantic, provincial King James succeeded to the throne. Dr John Dee was an ally of Satan, declared the royal expert in witchcraft, and all his posts were therefore forfeit. Despite his advanced age, Dee reacted violently, pointing to his long service with the Crown, demanding to be openly tried as a witch. Shabbily, James 1 refused any such trial: his reason for ejecting Dee from his sinecures was probably as much economical as moral, and John Dee had proved more than once his ability to wriggle out of a legal accusation. Left in a kind of limbo, deemed neither innocent nor proved guilty of forbidden practices, the old man retired to his small estate at Mortlake and there, in 1608, he died at the age of eighty-one.

The most sympathetic observer of Dee's career can come to hardly any other conclusion but that it was, at best, tatterdemalion. It seems scarcely possible that he could have joined with Kelly in raising the dead and transmuting gold without some suspicion that they were engaged in criminal, or near-criminal, deception of the gullible. Dee was, admittedly, remarkably short-sighted in many matters: he does not seem to have appreciated, for example, the significance of Kelly's cropped ears. But he was no fool, even though he seems to have been capable of a high degree of self-delusion. His quest for the philosophers' stone was not necessarily foolish or cynical: thousands of honourable men who could reasonably be dignified with the title of chemist had followed that same quest and indirectly contributed much to science.

Dee's complex character is rendered even more confusing in that Elizabeth trusted him. Predisposed as she was to the occult generally, her testimony regarding Dee's paranormal gifts is of no particular value. But as a politician and a judge of human nature she knew no superior and very few equals. The fact that she entrusted Dee with many delicate secret negotiations is unimpeachable testimony to his intelligence and general, normal, ability. Groping through the mists of nearly four centuries, hampered and tantalised by the fact that no one ever troubled to write a full-length biography of the man, although many mentioned him, the twentieth century observer is left with a handful of seemingly contradictory facts. Dee was a scholar and a statesman – who could yet descend to the cheapest of fairground huckstering and deceptions. He was on familiar terms with the great Queen of England – yet he could make a friend and colleague of a small-time crook like Edward Kelly. He could write *Divers Annotations and Inventions added after the Tenth Book of Euclid* – and also an account of his relationship with the spirit world, in particular the great angels Uriel and Michael. How, then, to resolve these seemingly irreconcilable elements? A tentative solution to the problem is that Dee possessed a faculty similar to that which J. W. Dunne possessed but that, where Dunne, working in the twentieth century, sought a rational explanation for the faculty, Dee, inevitably predisposed by his own period's beliefs, sought an explanation in the occult world. Kelly acted as some kind of catalyst and it was unfortunate for the scholarly, dignified Dr John Dee that his indispensable colleague also happened to be a petty criminal.

Six years after John Dee died in London, there was born in Derbyshire a child who was destined to be the last of the astrologers of the older, freer tradition in Britain. That tradition was to continue on in the American colonies, and later in the infant States of America. But in Europe, increasing scepticism undermined the hitherto secure status of the astrologer. It may have been a result of increased education; it may have arisen from a simple reaction against the intangible, against an age of unquestioning faith. But from whatever cause the astrologer was forced to abandon his pretensions of walking with kings, and was obliged indeed to keep the common touch, fighting for his living in the very gutter along with palmists, tinkers, thimbleriggers and such disreputable folk.

William Lilly was born in Diseworth, Leicestershire, on 1st May 1602. His father belonged to the minor country gentry, and young Lilly was fortunate to receive, as a result, what amounted to a respectable classical education whose emphasis upon Latin, Greek and Hebrew was to be useful in later years. His father, however, lurched from financial crisis to crisis, and Lilly was barely eighteen years of age when final and irrevocable ruin overwhelmed the family, with Lilly senior thrust into prison for debt. His son reacted to domestic disaster in a traditional manner. Putting a spare pair of shoes in his bag he began the long walk to London, the great city whose streets were paved with gold – for the fortunate.

Lilly belonged to the fortunate. He was clearly a pliable, glib youth with a highly-developed ability to be in the right place at the right time and with a winning smile of precisely sufficient warmth. His first master died – but left young Lilly an annuity of £20 a year. His master's widow, who must have been able to pass for Lilly's grandmother, was so taken by the young man that she exchanged his status of apprentice for that of husband. Conveniently dying some five years later, she left Lilly property to the very handsome amount of £1,000 per annum. Lilly felt, reasonably, that he could afford to relax and turned to a study which had been attracting his attention over a number of years – the study of astrology.

Later, he claimed that it was the heightened tension between Charles I and Parliament which first turned his thoughts to that direction. 'I did carefully take notice of every grand action betwixt king and parliament, and did first then incline to believe that as all sublunary affairs depend on superior causes so there was a possibility of discovering them by the configurations of the superior planets.'

To do Lilly justice, he did not rush into print, as did so many of his colleagues in the occult. He appears to have spent at least fourteen years in earnest study before adding his contribution to the ocean of predictive manuals that was beginning to flood the Western world. It was not until April 1644 that he brought out his first book of prophecies, modestly entitled *Merlinus Anglicus Junior*, to be followed a few months later by the orotundity of *A Prophecy of the White King and Dreadful Deadman Explained*. Thereafter, his almanacs came out with increasing frequency, each licensed by the Stationers' Company, which granted an indication of respectability in return for an automatic share of the profits.

William Lilly was to go down to posterity – even to that portion of it which mocked the very idea of star-gazing – as the astrologer who was fortunate enough to predict the Great Fire of London. Unlike many such predictions, it can be proved to have been written out, and actually in print, some time before the event. It was in 1648 that his *Astrological Predictions* carried a description which it is extremely difficult to fault:

In the year 1665 the Aphelium of Mars, who is the general signification of England, will be in Virgo, which is assuredly the ascendant of the English monarchy, but Aries of the Kingdom. When the absis therefore of Mars shall appear in Virgo who shall expect less than a strange catastrophe of human affairs in the commonwealth, monarchy and king-dom of England. There will then, either in or about those times, or near that year, or within ten years, more or less of

21 William Lilly's symbolised drawing of the Fire of London. Gemini is the sign of the City of London

that time, appear in this kingdom so strange a revolution of fate, so grand a catastrophe and great mutation unto this monarchy and government as never yet appeared of which as the times now stand, I have no liberty or encouragement to deliver my opinion – only it will be ominous to London, unto her merchants at sea, to her traffique on land, to her poor, to all sorts of people, inhabiting in her or to her liberties, by reason of sundry fires and a consuming plague.

He returned to the theme three years later, illustrating it with ' the representation of people in their winding sheets, persons digging graves and sepultures, coffins, etc.'

If the fire and plague had not struck London in 1665 and 1666 there would have been nothing particularly noteworthy in that paragraph. The great part of it seems to be ordinary padding, although to a fellow astrologer it would presumably have been a legitimate sketch of the astrological framework in which the event occurred. The author, too, is almost pathologically cautious regarding the chronology – ' either in or about those times, or near that year, or within ten years more or less '. One is left with the inescapable impression that if the Great Fire had not occurred in the decade 1665-75 Lilly would simply have shrugged and claimed that it would occur sometime in the next ten years, or the ten after that. But equally inescapable is the fact that the twin catastrophes of fire and plague occurred precisely as he predicted.

Two years before the plague struck London, and while Lilly's prediction was merely one of an untold number, a vicious attack was launched upon him by a fellow astrologer. ' There needs not much skill in his pretended art to discover the vanity of it ', announced a certain Thomas Gataker, BD, in a pamphlet entitled *Against the scurrilous aspersions of that Grand Imposter Mr William Lillie*. In the same year that the plague occurred, he was under attack again from a different quarter and for a wholly different reason. Gataker had denounced him as an impostor and now, as Lilly himself recorded : ' I was indicted by a half-witted young woman for that I had given judgement upon stolen goods and received 2s 6d.' And this was said to be contrary unto an Act in King James's time made. It appeared that he had used Satanic arts to defraud the young woman out of her 2s 6d for she claimed ' that she had been several times with me and that afterwards she could not rest at nights, but was troubled with bears, lions and tygers etc.'

And at last William Lilly was justified, his astrological prediction substantiated when first bubonic plague swept through London and then, by a fortunate dispensation, fire roared in its wake to cleanse the filthy streets. But it did the unfortunate William Lilly little good at the time. After the flames had died down and a dazed population was creeping back into the blackened shell of the once-great city, a Committee of Parliament came across his prediction. It seemed so exact, corresponding so closely to what really happened – in particular that remarkable double-barrelled prophecy regarding the fire that would follow the plague – that it seemed only too possible a case for arson. He was summoned before the Committee and questioned closely, some believing that he had been bribed to arson by a foreign power, others that he had committed it on his own initiative in order that his prophecy might be fulfilled. It proved impossible to substantiate either accusation and Lilly was dismissed with, perhaps, the most impressive testimony a prophet had ever been granted.

Lilly never again brought off such a remarkable shot but its fame made his reputation for the rest of his life. Later, he skilfully bolstered his astrological predictions with a shrewd knowledge of current affairs. Success seems to have turned him into a kind of Polonius, judging by his *Epistle to the Student of Astrology* where the aspiring astrologer is urged to be ' humane, curtius, familiar to all, easie of access. Afflict not the miserable with terror of a harsh judgement : direct such to call on God, to divert his judgements impending over them. Be civil, sober, covet not an estate. Give freely to the poor, let no worldly wealth procure an erroneous judgement from thee.'

Lilly certainly had no humble ideas of the station of the astrologer, for such advice could as properly be given to a young prince. It was this pomposity, this effortless assumption of superiority that was, in part, responsible for the barbed attacks made upon him.

> Mr Lilly in all these dreadful Eclipses and malignant Aspects finds much matter of bad, dismal and disastrous concernment to Princes, Potentates, Priests, Lawyers, Husbandmen, Graziers, etc., but none at all to Wizards, Witches, Conjurers, Fortune-tellers, Sorcerers, Stargazers, Astrologers, etc. No malignity of any aspect belike is able to reach them.

But it was only in part. From this time forward there is evident an increasingly bitter rivalry between 'professional' astrologers, a rivalry produced by the fact that the printing press had abruptly widened the field available for financial cultivation and more and more fortune-tellers were hastening in to exploit it.

It was out of this welter of accusation and counter-accusation that one of the most joyous of literary hoaxes came into being at the hand of no less a person than Jonathan Swift. His target was a certain John Partridge, who was making a comfortable living by publishing astrological almanacs. It is difficult to say why Swift picked on this particular man, for Partridge seems to be no worse than others of his 'profession' unless, perhaps, it was his tendency to use his predictions to bolster up his own political prejudices. Whatever the reason, Swift swung into the attack with his own deadpan *Predictions for the year 1708*, allegedly made by Isaac Bickerstaff.

> My first prediction is but a trifle [the almanac announced]. Yet I will make it to show how ignorant these sottish pretenders to astrology are in their own concerns. It relates to Partridge the almanac maker. I have consulted the star of

his nativity by my own rules and find he will infallibly die upon the 29th of March next, about eleven at night, of a raging fever. Therefore I advise him to consider of it, and settle his affairs in time.

'Isaac Bickerstaff's' publication seemed as honest and straightforward as any of its contemporaries and the majority of those who bought it took his prediction regarding Partridge perfectly seriously. Partridge protested vigorously, but the joke had not ended. When the fatal day had come and gone 'Isaac Bickerstaff' published yet another pamphlet, *An account of the death of Mr Partridge, the Almanac maker, upon the 29th Instant, in a letter from a Revenue Officer to a Person of Honour*. Poor Partridge's life was thereafter made miserable by an endless stream of practical jokers, some of whom demanded payment for his coffin and burial. More seriously, the Stationers' Hall seems to have been taken in by Swift's pamphlet and solemnly removed Partridge's name from their rolls, causing him real financial loss. He was forced to the extreme lengths of advertising the fact that he was neither dead nor sleeping, but alive and hoping to continue practising as a seer into the future.

It would be too much to claim that Swift's pamphlet mocked astrology into silence but it came at just the right moment to have an impressive effect. Superstition and belief in the occult generally had changed its direction rather than its form, but this was, after all, the Age of Reason and in that light astrology seemed painfully thin and fragile. On the Continent a curiously similar event to the 'Bickerstaff' prophecy had also helped to mock astrology off the stage. Two astrologers had independently predicted the death of Voltaire at the age of 32; at the age of 66 Voltaire published his own pamphlet humbly apologising for proving astrology incorrect by continuing to draw breath. The art, or craft, or pseudo-science had had a long reign since its revival in the twelfth century: it had endured the traumatic discoveries of Coper-

nicus and Brahe, Kepler and Galileo. It would probably even
have survived the work of Isaac Newton – there were some,
indeed, who claimed that even this ice-cold philosopher held a
warm regard for astrology. But the intellectual climate of the
eighteenth century was altogether against the belief. It sank
down in to the despised lower strata of society, again becoming
the property of conjurers and thimbleriggers and fairground
charlatans, earning pennies from the lowly instead of crowns
from the great.

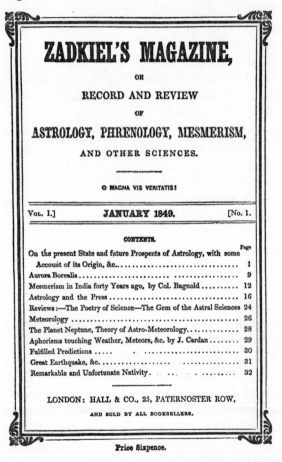

ZADKIEL'S MAGAZINE,

OR

RECORD AND REVIEW

OF

ASTROLOGY, PHRENOLOGY, MESMERISM,

AND OTHER SCIENCES.

O MAGNA VIS VERITATIS!

VOL. I.]   **JANUARY 1849.**   [No. 1.

CONTENTS.

LONDON: HALL & CO., 25, PATERNOSTER ROW,

AND SOLD BY ALL BOOKSELLERS.

Price Sixpence.

22. Title page of the first issue of Zadkiel's Magazine

Chapter 7
The Nineteenth-Century Revival

Throughout the three millennia of its recorded existence the reputation of astrology has risen and fallen, in a series of great waves and troughs, without any apparent relationship to outside causes. There is no immediately detectable affinity between the fifth and the eighteenth centuries, when astrology was in total dispute. There is even less affinity between the first and twentieth centuries when the once-despised art again came into its own in the popular field.

The eighteenth and early nineteenth century saw astrology in a totally debased state in Europe. In Britain, however, there was a continuous thread which linked the heyday of Renaissance astrology with the lush flowering that took place in the 1890s. The almanacs published by the seventeenth century astrologers continued to appear, year by year. It seems unlikely that the British were inherently more superstitious than the French or the Germans or the Scandinavians and the probability is that the continued publication was a direct result of the existence of the Stationers' Company. The Company had a monopoly in astrological almanacs and it was a relatively simple task to engage some hack to keep the more popular almanacs up to date year after year. The most famous of these almanacs – whose name at least was destined to survive into the present period – was the *Vox Stellarum* of Francis Moore who died in 1715. The *Merlinus Liberatus* of

G

23 Illustration from Raphael's *Almanac* for 1824, later claimed
as predicting the death of Louis XVIII

the maligned John Partridge also survived his death and
continued on into the nineteenth century. Such almanacs
belonged unblushingly to the lowest strata of their ' craft '.
Already surviving astrologers were drawing apart into two
main groups, the predictive who had every intention of
making what profit they could from the gullible of every class,
and the speculative who looked down upon their commercially
grubby brothers and strove to raise astrology into the higher
realms. But it was the predictors who probably kept interest in
the craft alive with their flimsy pamphlets and very cloudy
personal horoscopes.

In 1784 there appeared an immensely ambitious work from
one of the speculative astrologers. This was *The Celestial Art*

of Astrology by Ebenezer Sibley, a physician whose interest in astrology was reasonably pure of financial influence but did not, thereby, automatically endear him to his astrological colleagues. They regarded him, frankly, as a quack – a man who had come late to the ancient and royal art and sought to make his name by stealing the work of other men. Much of the *Celestial Art* did indeed come straight from other books but Sibley could reasonably claim that he was merely acting as an editor for material which would probably have been lost otherwise. The interested could find in his book a large number of horoscopes not only of great men – including Christ – but of countries. One of the very attractive illustrations showed the Angel of the Revolution flying over America, displaying a horoscope cast for the Declaration of Independence in 1776. The picture also incidentally illustrated a typical astrologer's advertising technique. The displayed horoscope was impressive in its details and in its accuracy: its only drawback, from a predictionable viewpoint, was the fact that it was drawn up eight years after the event.

The first two decades of the nineteenth century in England was marked by little activity. There were a few horoscopes of Napoleon, most of them based on the same kind of wishful thinking which disposed of Adolf Hitler during the Second World War. John Worsdale, in his *Celestial Philosophy,* amassed an impressive number of cases where his prediction – always dire – came true. In one of them, where he predicted death by drowning, there may have been a similar, unconscious attraction to water as had caused the death by suicide of Pierleoni of Spoleto. As Worsdale tells the story with much self-congratulation, a young girl – Mary Dickson – asked him to predict the time of her marriage. ' I answered that I was confident that she would never enter into the matrimonial union. She said she was sorry that I should give such a false judgement, as she expected to marry in the ensuing Spring. I then informed her that *something* of an *awful nature* would occur, before the month of March, then next ensuing, which would destroy Life.' The girl laughed in his face and, with ill-concealed relish the prophet informed her that ' *Drowning* would be the cause of her dissolution '. Unsurprisingly he ended his account with the statement that, despite his repeated warnings, ' she insisted on travelling by water, fell in, and was drowned.' No actuary ever swore to this series of events so there is no means of knowing whether poor Mary's horoscope was of the same nature as that of the Declaration of Independence – accurate, detailed, impressive but compiled after, instead of before, the event.

Until now, astrological predictions and the drawing up of horoscopes had been done in decent privacy. The client would first have to find his astrologer, then either visit him, or invite him to his home, and provide the essential information. The print-hungry nineteenth century was to change this traditional approach. Throughout the century a wide variety of crafts and professions discovered that they could appeal to a vastly increased audience through the media of cheap pamphlets or part publications and it was therefore inevitable that astrology would exploit this enormous market.

The man who was to launch mass-produced astrology on to the unsuspecting public arrived in London in 1820. He was Robert Cross Smith, a native of Bristol, come to London like so many young men, to make his fortune. London at that period was an excellent place for a young man with the ability to spin words, the stamina to do so for twelve hours a day or more and the modesty to expect only a pittance for his work. Smith developed an interest in astrology and, in due course, found himself installed in the editor's chair of a publication with the engaging title of *The Straggling Astrologer of the Nineteenth Century*. Smith hoped to tempt the public with a real, live princess on the editorial board – the lady who claimed to be the daughter of the Duke of Cumberland and went under the title of HRH The Princess Olive of Cumberland. He created rather more effective publicity by launching what was to prove the first regular series of predictions for his

24 Horoscope of the American Revolution, an illustration from
Silbey's *Celestial Science of Astrology*

25 The occult begins to permeate astrology : illustration from a
nineteenth-century astrological textbook

readers – the first of the great wave of popular astrological almanacs.

The Straggling Astrologer failed but, with the survival skill of the hack, Smith found himself shortly afterwards at the editorial desk of a publication calling itself *The Prophetic Messenger*. He adopted for it the same regular series of predictions and chose for himself a pseudonym – Raphael. Over the next few decades there were to be many resounding pseudonyms for astrologers, most of them taking their names from the higher members of the Hebrew pantheon but 'Raphael's Almanac' was to transcend its creator and become a household word. When Smith died – still a young man – in 1832, his pupil and successor John Palmer adopted the name of 'Raphael'; others were to follow suit until the name became a species of title. As far as the public was concerned 'Raphael' must have seemed as invulnerable to time as he was prolific in words.

Smith was, essentially, the hack astrologer, producing material that would sell, possibly – or even probably – believing in what he did but preoccupied in making a living rather than unveiling occult truths. Far different was the other popular astrological journalist of the period – Richard Morrison, who copied Smith in writing under a resounding pseudonym, 'Zadkiel'.

Smith had painfully climbed upwards from very obscure origins: Morrison, if anything, descended in the world. His background was solid middle class and he himself was a half-pay lieutenant of the Royal Navy. Admittedly, he left the Navy in 1815 when he was only twenty-one and never again troubled to go to sea, but no one could deny him the title of officer of the Royal Navy. To do him justice, he made little use of his official standing and while he lived, with reasonable success, as a professional astrologer for nearly sixty years, he seems to have adopted the profession as a vocation and not simply as a means of making an uncertain living. A burly, confident-looking man who did indeed have something

of the seadog about him, he did not hesitate to correct Isaac
Newton and elaborated his own system of the universe, over-
toppling the new-fangled heliocentric system and placing the
Earth again in its natural and divinely ordained position in
the centre of the cosmos. He probably entered astrology
though his association with Smith, who had founded a small,
very elite society called the Mercurii. Its members very likely
had no choice but to be an elite for there is no indication that
many had ever heard of the society, but it served to spark off
Morrison's ambition. Unlike many – and probably the
majority – of the sorry crew who turned to astrology in the
eighteenth and nineteenth centuries, Morrison was not merely
formally educated but was a man of lively curiosity and wide
if eccentric culture. He had read deeply, could write with
great zest and vividness and could have earned a better living
in some other section of the Grub Street jungle. But astrology
had attracted him and he remained faithful to it, even though
it was necessary to keep ' Zadkiel ' in a totally different com-
partment to ' Lieutenant Richard Morrison ' at such a lowly
pass had astrology arrived.

The latter part of the nineteenth century was distinguished
both in Britain and the USA by a steep rise in the study of
occultism. At one extreme the study could be concerned with
such a sober subject as the evaluation of mesmerism and
telepathy; at the other extreme it touched the Gothic fantasies
of Spiritualism. Astrology was deeply affected by it and it was
from approximately this period that its practitioners fell into
one of two camps. There were the purists – those who believed
it possible that astrology should be classed as a science and
who despised and deplored the antics of their less dignified
colleagues. And there were those who firmly regarded astrology as a branch of the ' occult '. Morrison belonged to the
latter school. He investigated the possibilities of crystal-gazing
or ' skrying '. He claimed that because his crystal was
controlled by Michael, archangel of the Sun, its potential was
far greater than the smaller, commoner kinds. He published in

his almanac details of the communications he had received from the Other World via his crystal and succeeded in arousing the interest of the Quality so that, for a few months, crystal-gazing became all the rage in Kensington and Belgravia.

But astrology was his dominant interest. His almanac reached a circulation of 60,000 copies annually but his stock as a private consultant also soared. He was able to demand – and get – up to £10 for a private consultation, and claimed thereby that he was doing astrology a great service, for people tended to value higher that which cost more. He was, in fact, rather too accurate for his own good. The 1861 edition of *Zadkiel's Almanac* carried a warning regarding the health of the Prince Consort. The unfortunate Albert died at the end of that year and the coincidence created speculation. A century or so earlier and the successful prophet would have been hauled before a court of enquiry to establish just how he knew the death of a royal personage was likely to happen. As it was, Zadkiel merely had to endure the tongue-lashing of the press. The *Daily Telegraph* succinctly summed up the same sceptical view of philosophy as Pico della Mirandola had done three centuries before.

> Once in every five years or so, one of Zadkiel's prophecies, which are generally the stupidest jumping at probable eventualities, may by an accident come true. Whereupon the seer goes into raptures of the ' Right Again !' description, and sells his almanacs, we are sorry to learn, by the thousand ! . . . We might pass this rubbishing pamphlet by with contempt, but the publicity it has recently attained demands that it and its author should be exposed and denounced. The one is a sham, the other is a swindler.

Strong words, but even stronger were to follow. ' Who is this Zadkiel?' the *Telegraph* had demanded rhetorically, and the morning's post brought them the answer from no less a personality than a Rear-Admiral of the Royal Navy who informed the world that Lieutenant Morrison, Zadkiel's alter ego, 'has not served afloat since 1815' – a little matter of forty-seven years ago.

A friend of mine reminds me that the author of *Zadkiel* is the celebrated crystal globe seer who gulled many of our nobility about the year 1852. Making use of a boy under fourteen or a girl under twelve he pretended, by their looking into the crystal globe, to hold converse with the spirits of the Apostles – even our Saviour, with all the angels of light as well as darkness, and to tell what was going on in any part of the world. One noble lady gave the boy £5 to give her intelligence regarding her boy, who was in the Mediterranean.

Zadkiel had no choice but to sue the gallant admiral for libel. A sceptical jury found for him – to the tune of damages of 20s and no costs.

In 1875 there was launched in New York the newest and dizziest of the 'occult societies' which mushroomed during the second half of the century. The society was the Theosophical Society and its founder was Helena Paulovna Blavatsky. 'In personal appearance the "old one", as Madame was familiarly described by her following, has been described as globular in shape, with dull grey complexion, a far from an attractive physiognomy and eyes like discoloured turquoises,' an ungallant article described her shortly after her death. But behind that unprepossessing exterior was an ebullient personality, a keen if unscrupulous mind and a will-power that could bulldoze its way over any opposition.

Helena Blavatsky was born, née Hahn, in Ekaterinaslav, Russia, in 1831. She was only seventeen when she married Blavatsky, a Russian official, and the marriage lasted no more than a few months. Later, when virginity seemed to be a useful occult possession, she claimed that the unfortunate Nicephore Blavatsky had been 'a plumeless raven nearer seventy than sixty' – which would have made him at least 110 years old at his death. It was this kind of blatant juggling with the truth which disconcerted Madame Blavatsky's friends, delighted her enemies and gave Theosophy its distinctive flavour.

Between 1848 and 1858 – from her seventeenth to her twenty-seventh year – Helena Blavatsky's movements are obscure. She was to romanticise that decade as the 'veiled' period of her life and there were later many, but studiously vague, references to residence in Tibet and the Himalayas generally. She visited Russia in the 1860s and gained considerable publicity as a medium but it was in America in the early 1870s that she really shot to fame – or, at least, acquired that sensational publicity which she was never to lose. This was the time when Spiritualism suddenly burst over the USA, releasing a shower of mediums and triggering off an almost hysterical controversy, as the defenders and the attackers of the occult ranged themselves to do battle on behalf of reason, or of Eternal Truth, depending upon which side their preferences lay.

Helena Blavatsky energetically threw herself on the side of Eternal Truth. But not for her were the plumbers and pedlars who constituted the controls in the Beyond for most of her sister mediums. Instead, she announced that her controls were actually still in the world of the living, although removed some thousands of miles distant from her. They were the 'mahatmas', or sages, known as Koot Hoomi and Morya, comfortably established among their native snows in Tibet and conversing with her by means of their astral bodies. Madame Blavatsky was an adept of that philosophy known to Barnum and Joseph Goebbels, among others: the bigger the claim and the wilder the illusion, the more likely was the public to accept it. One clergyman solemnly deposed how Madame Blavatsky went alone into a suburban garden to await a reply from her sages in Tibet. A few moments later she re-entered the house, carrying in her hand a letter which had magically appeared in a tree, wafted there across the planet by the power of her Tibetan friends. The reader is torn between astonishment at the naïvety of the ' observer ' and admiration for the unbounded confidence of the lady herself.

It was this immense confidence which enabled her to act as a kind of rallying point for the occultists of America. The contact with the Beyond which had started with the Foxe sisters had not ushered in a world of universal peace but one of increasing noise and acrimony as the spiritualist groups fragmented and bitterly warred one with the other. Here was a potent force being dissipated – until the coming of Helena Blavatsky. Spiritualism was in error, she announced stridently – but so were the materialists. Truth lay in – Tibet, Burma, India, Egypt, anywhere but in the country where they were discussing it. Two years later she brought out her *Isis Un-veiled,* following it up with the *Secret Doctrine.* Textbooks of the Theosophist movement, both works were heavily based on unacknowledged quotations of other people's work. The underlying ideal was the ancient, noble and impossible ideal of the synthesis – of the drawing together in one framework the essence of human religious experience. As with the majority of occultists, Helena Blavatsky was dazzled by the Far East, wholly ignoring the immense mystic tradition in Christianity. But Christianity was commonplace, familiar to the most ordinary people while initiation into the complexities of Brahmanism and Buddhism was reserved for the few, creating a comforting feeling of being among the elite.

Helena Blavatsky unerringly chose the superficial, the obviously glamorous and esoteric but she had as unerring an instinct for what the public liked and wanted. Brahmanism and Buddhism provided her society with a technical language, its doctrines were an extraordinary fruit salad of ancient Egyptian, cabbalistic, astrological, occultistic, Indian, and Chaldean teaching, simplified and codified to fit in with the new cult. Mastering the teachings of Theosophy gave the neophytes the maximum sense of achieving wisdom for the minimum outlay in intellectual expenditure.

Astrology benefited immediately from Theosophy, and on two distinct counts. The new cult was socially acceptable in a way astrology had not been for over two centuries. Throughout living memory its practice had been in the hands either of grubby little men and women hopefully trying to turn a reasonably honest penny, or of such as Morrison and Smith. And while Zadkiel and Raphael enjoyed a considerable following in the servants' hall, they were still by no means welcomed in the drawing-room. But Theosophy could be, and Theosophy, in the person of its ebullient, derided but immensely influential mistress, had ' amply proved that even horoscopes and judiciary astrology are not quite based on fiction, and that stars and constellations have an occult and mysterious influence on, and connection with, individuals '.

Equally as important as the social cachet granted astrology by Theosophy was the technical assistance given in the embarrassing matter of the new planets. Astrology, from its remotest beginnings, had been firmly founded on the septizonium, the ' seven stars in the sky '. It is probably from this that seven, as a lucky number, has entered the majority of cultures, both primitive and sophisticated. Then, in 1781, William Herschel discovered a planet beyond the Orbit of Saturn. He wanted to call it ' Georgium Sidus ' in a not very subtle flattery of George III of England, who happened to be his patron. Others wanted to call it ' Herschel ' – and Raphael, in fact, referred to it under this name. But the etiquette of international astronomy fortunately prevailed over national pride and the new planet joined its brethren in the catalogues under the classical name of Uranus.

The initial reaction of astrologers to this naked fact of life was to ignore it, arguing that because it could not be seen by the naked eye it could have no effect upon human affairs. But it was second nature among astrologers to look for ' correspondences ' and gradually Uranus was drawn into the scheme of things and given the characteristics of eccentricity and leadership. But no sooner had astrologers tidied up the situation than the restless astronomers, armed with bigger and ever more effective telescopes, discovered yet another planet in 1846. The classical tradition having been successfully defended in the case of Uranus, the new planet was accordingly given the name of yet another god – Neptune – and endowed with his watery characteristic.

But by now the astrologers were becoming punch-drunk. How many more planets were there to be discovered, and what effect did this have on their time-honoured system of the septizonium? None at all, boomed Madame Blavatsky, Indian astrology postulated no less than twelve planets, one for each sign of the Zodiac, and Indian astrology had received the blessing of Theosophy.

The degree of respectability which astrology had attained, in Britain at least, was well demonstrated by the fact that one of its open adherents in the 1880s was Richard Garnett, scholar, author and Keeper of Printed Books in the British Museum. Garnett rejected the occult and mystical view of astrology. He claimed, indeed, that it was – or should be – one of the most exact of the sciences for it depended wholly on the most rigorous and exact of mathematical calculations. He seems to have regarded it less as an attempt to predict the future as an attempt to classify and codify the myriad aspects of human personality in one all-embracing system. It was the beginning of a new look in astrology, one which, in a few decades time, could use the fashionable term ' psychology ' to bolster up its claims. Curiously, at about the time that Garnett was attempting to assess character by astrology, and hence predict the possibilities of action produced by character tendencies, the founder of psychology itself was toying with astrology. Sigmund Freud's interest was only indirect, arising from his friendship with Wilhelm Fliess, a fellow physician. Fliess, commonly dismissed as a crank, had not, in fact, fallen for any heresy more radical than the ancient problem of correspondences. He shared to the full the passionate curiosity of the nineteenth century scientist, a curiosity which, coupled with immense self-confidence, was to lead many of them down curious byways of the occult. Fliess' particular aberration was Pythagorean numerology, an aberration which led him imperceptibly to seek some causal relationship between the movements of the planets and the rhythms of human metabolism. He found none – certainly none to convince his friend and temporary disciple Freud, but ironically Freud's own pupil, Jung, was later to investigate astrology and evolve that theory of synchronicity which was to give much comfort to late twentieth century astrologers seeking the blessing of the twentieth century priests of wisdom, the scientists.

Shortly before Madame Blavatsky died in London in 1891, a member of her Inner Group brought to her meetings a young man who was to carry the cause of Theosophical astrology into the twentieth century, and incidentally make a good profit out of it. His name was William Allen, his profession was that of commercial traveller, but he had definite ambitions to do rather better for himself. Astrology, as propounded by the legendary confidant of the Tibetan sages seemed a more likely path to a gracious way of life than tramping the roads with his suitcase of samples. But William Allen scarcely needed Madame Blavatsky's exhortations to adopt Theosophy and the occult. He early abandoned his prosaic name and was thereafter known as Alan Leo. He had lived before, he announced, confidently dragging astrology back into the amorphous world of the occult. But he succeeded in impressing not only fellow astrologers but the rather less susceptible bankers and printers to finance and publish yet another astrological magazine. His partner was F. W. Lacey, who wrote under the name of Aphorel – the resounding names were back, with Charubel, Casael, Sepharial rubbing shoulders in prosaic London. Shortly after becoming an editor – a craft he knew nothing about – Leo became a husband which was also a craft he knew nothing about. His wife, Bessie, was a fervent Theosophist and, as a condition of marriage, had insisted that it should be entirely platonic. Leo agreed to all terms: he allowed Bessie to interfere in the magazine and actually to write for it. Yet, remarkably, *Modern Astrology* not only survived but actually flourished, possibly because all concerned with the magazine had no journalistic experience, and so had no preconceived ideas as to what the public ought to want. They were, themselves, representative members of the public and instinctively chose what they themselves wanted. And what the public wanted, it seemed, were cheap horoscopes by the hundred – by the thousand.

Thirty years earlier the great Zadkiel had stoutly insisted that any astrologer worth his trade should charge in guineas rather than shillings. And hitherto, all but the most debased of market-place astrologers had at least paid lip service to the idea of discharging a unique function for each of their clients, erecting each horoscope *ab ovo* from material obtained specifically for that purpose. Leo dispensed with this requirement and made a modest fortune by so doing. For the payment of a shilling, readers of his magazine were entitled to their own horoscope. The editorial offices were overwhelmed with postal orders and demands for the horoscopes and, to cope, he employed a temporary staff of astrologers to churn out the horoscopes. Between 1900 and 1903 he probably made £1,000 clear profit on these shilling horoscopes alone – a sum worth ten times as much in today's currency. He did not escape wholly unscathed. He was twice charged with fortune-telling and was fined £25 on the second occasion. But almost until his death in 1917 his astrological factory was in full blast. The shilling horoscopes came to an end in 1903, but there were still the individual horoscopes to be cast and in addition was his prodigious output of astrological literature. Most of it was designed for the Do-It-Yourself market and, in theory, should have put the professional astrologer out of business. But among the thousands who learned to erect their own horoscopes, hundreds were bitten by the astrological bug and came back for more.

Leo's death put a brief term to the reviving craft. Curiously although astrology flourished vigorously in the Second World War, it had no such fortune in the First. It may have been due to the lack of outstanding practitioners; it may have been that the revival of formal religion under the stress of war pushed into the background the more glamorous but flimsier cults. From whatever cause, in Europe, at least, the majority of astrologers put away their charts as the lamps went out over the Continent.

29 Alan Leo, astrologer and theosophist, depicted within his own horoscope

Chapter 8
Astrology in the Modern World

The Sun in Scorpio squares Pluto in ascending Leo. The Sun rules Leo : Pluto rules Scorpio. The Sun is life ruler and asterisks the cusp of its own 5th House while Pluto ascends in the all-important 1st House of the personality.

The quotation, part of an astrological study of the present Prince of Wales, is taken not from a technical publication intended only for practising astrologers but from a mass circulation magazine, freely available at all bookstalls and intended for the general public. The editors are confident that a financially significant proportion of the population are sufficiently well-versed in the arcane jargon to make such a publication commercially viable. There are no indications that they might be in error : to the contrary. Ten years ago, the magazine in question was a modest affair of newsprint – little more than a glorified pamphlet : today it is a glossy – well illustrated, well produced and, for the cognoscenti, well written. Astrology is, in the last third of the twentieth century, enjoying a boom such as has not been known since the late sixteenth century.

The beginning of the boom can conveniently be placed in April 1930, when the American astrologer Evangeline Adams began broadcasting – the first ' radio astrologer '. The United States, which traditionally swooped on to all novel ideas, had been curiously tardy in displaying much interest in astrology.

In the seventeenth century Increase Mather, the parson son of the great Cotton Mather, had looked upon the comet of 1680 as a divine warning of coming tribulation and so announced it in an impassioned series of sermons.

> The floods of great water are coming. I am persuaded that God is about to open the windows of heaven and to pour down the cataracts of his wrath ere this generation is passed away. Let us then prepare for trouble, for the Lord has fired his beacon in the heavens.

The beacon in the heavens continued on its enormous journey, the much-threatened, much-harried Earth somehow continued to survive and both Increase Mather and his admiring parishioners put the somewhat embarrassing prophecy out of their minds.

The few astrological practitioners in America during the eighteenth and nineteenth centuries shared the same malaise as affected their counterparts in Europe. When at last the craft was again revived it was under the aegis of outright charlatans or mystagogues for whom the ancient craft was merely another version of the occult, a more elegant form of table-rapping, perhaps, or another, compendious philosophy in which reincarnation and increased business efficiency could be slotted without too much trouble.

American astrologers tended to turn to Europe for encouragement, information and technical instruction but in the first decade of the twentieth century an enterprising Dane, Max Heindel, arrived in New York with a briefcase full of papers, a glib tongue, and a belief that there was money in the occult. In Berlin, Heindel had attended the lectures of Rudolph Steiner, the anthroposophist. Steiner had been the founder of the German section of Theosophy but as the movement grew ever wilder under the successor to Madame Blavatsky, he seceded and founded his own 'Wisdom of Humanity' society. It bore a strong family resemblance to its Theosophical parent in that it was eclectic, seeking to draw

H

together and classify scores of elements supposedly common to all cultures; it differed radically from Theosophy in its intellectual content. Steiner and his followers were prepared to place their findings under normal scientific assessment, sparing the necessity of belief in letters that arrived magically from Tibet.

In America, Max Heindel predictably joined the Theosophical movement – or, rather, a breakaway section of it called the Universal Brotherhood. But even this schism did not satisfy him and he, in his turn, founded an occult society – the Rosicrucians. In tracing the dizzy careers of the occultists it is seldom clear what are their motives in forming yet another society with a unique key to the Ultimate Truths. It would seem that a powerful motive of Heindel's was the straightforwardly financial. The hungry sheep of his Rosicrucian Fellowship were fed with ' Master's Letters ', epistles guiding them through the perilous, exciting paths of the occult, written by Max Heindel – and drawing very heavily indeed on the Rudolph Steiner lectures he had attended in Berlin. Apart from the letters were his copious contributions to astrological literature. His *Message of the Stars* enjoyed an immense success. Colourful and imprecise, it gave the reader an illusion of being drawn into an arcanum, titillated the permanent human desire for impending doom, but also reassured him that the guardians would yet protect.

What success in prediction – if any – that Heindel enjoyed cannot now be assessed, so buried is it under a mass of words. Evangeline Adams was in a wholly different category – if only because her claims were tested in a lawcourt and triumphed. Her debut in New York was dramatic enough : she warned the owner of her hotel that he was threatened with imminent disaster and the hotel was burned down on the following day. The luck or prescience attracted attention – it was not, after all, bad publicity for the hotelier who probably had a hand in the ensuing fuss around Evangeline Adams. She handled it adroitly and gained so wide a reputation that the attention of the police was attracted. In America, as in Britain, fortune-telling was illegal and, for the police, casting nativities differed not the slightest from reading tea-leaves or peering into crystal balls. She defended herself so ably in court, however, that the judge went on record as saying that she had made a science out of a notoriously unstable art and discharged her. From that moment she never looked back. In 1930 she had her own radio programme. Part of its success was due to its Miss Lonelyhearts approach, conveying the standard advice and sympathy to the bewildered, the lonely, the bereaved. But its centre point were her astrological predictions both for individuals and the community and, at the height of her fame, she was receiving thousands of letters a day. One of the more remarkable of her claims was that she acted as astro-financial adviser to the millionaire J. P. Morgan. The ability to make a lot of money does not necessarily imply an immunity to superstition, but the claim seems unlikely if only because astrologers as a race would presumably be rather richer than they appear if it were possible to operate the Stock Exchange under the guidance of the stars.

Evangeline Adams died in 1932 and was given the kind of send-off usually reserved for film stars. Certainly the astrological fraternity in the States was deeply in her debt, the legal judgement of 1914 having conferred upon it the status at least of a profession, if not a science. The numbers of astrologers rose steadily in response: by 1941 there were at least 1,000 and by the late 1960s the registered number was more than 1,500, most of them working under the auspices of the American Federation of Astrologers, an association founded in 1928 with the avowed intention of divesting astrology as far as possible of its magical and occultistic trappings.

Until 1930 astrological prediction was still the product of a lengthy and tedious erection of personal horoscopes. Alan Leo's experiment in mass-produced nativities seems to have died with him. But it was destined for a resurrection and an astonishing new lease of life – a lease of life during which it has overshadowed all other forms so that, currently, for most people ' astrology ' means simply the column of ' predictions ' published daily or weekly in the popular press.

The new development can be dated precisely – 24th August 1931. The day was a Sunday and the editor of the *Sunday Express* had been faced with something of a problem – how to give a fresh slant on the news, already three days old, of the birth of a second daughter to the Duke and Duchess of York. Influenced, perhaps, by the Evangeline Adams radio success in New York, in London the *Express*'s editor contacted a professional astrologer and asked him to provide a horoscope for the young Princess Margaret. The astrologer was R. H. Naylor, a little man who looked like a schoolmaster and was later to earn qualified approval as the most accurate in his profession.

The article attracted considerable interest, containing as it did the two potent ingredients of royalty and occultism, and Naylor was invited to contribute another article the following week. In it, he mentioned that British aircraft were likely to be going through a dangerous period – and a few hours later the news of the R101 disaster broke. The *Sunday Express* not unnaturally made capital out of the astrologer's accuracy and modern, mass newspaper astrology was launched. Other popular newspapers rapidly followed suit: the picturesque Gypsy Petulengro signed up with the *Sunday Chronicle* complete with bandana and ear-rings; the more soberly-dressed Edward Lyndoe joined the *People*; the *Sunday Dispatch* availed itself of the services of W. J. Tucker. Simultaneously predictive manuals written by the better-known newspaper astrologers began again to appear on the market. In the 1970s they were to be numbered by the dozen, ranging from flimsy pamphlets to elaborate and expensive hardback books. In the 1930s they were still comparatively rare, requiring the name of a well-known astrologer to overcome the lingering remnants of public inertia.

The biggest blow which has struck predictive astrology in

26 Title-page of *The Astrologer of the Nineteenth Century*

THE ASTROLOGER,
of the Nineteenth Century,
OR THE
Master Key of Futurity,
being a Complete System of
ASTROLOGY, GEOMANCY & OCCULT SCIENCE.

I consider the heavens the work of thy fingers, the Moon and the Stars which thou hast ordained. Psal. viii. 3.

They fought from heaven, the Stars in their courses fought against Sisera. Judges v. 20.

Sidus adsit amicum. Cicero.

27 Madame Helena Blavatsky, founder of Theosophy

28 Evangeline Adams, the first 'radio astrologer'

modern times was the universal failure of all astrologers to predict the onset of the Second World War. Petulengro was later to claim that he had foreseen the fall of France but kept the news to himself so as not to dishearten his fellow countrymen and it may well be that the astrologers who did foresee the war kept quiet out of humanitarian terms. But lack of any evidence to the contrary forces the observer to the conclusions that the stargazers, to a man and a woman, somehow overlooked one of the most titanic events in human history. And the sceptical can be forgiven for wondering how the astrologers can spot minutiae and yet miss an event of this nature.

The dominant note in popular astrology, however, is that of good cheer. Things are eventually going to turn out all right : it's a long lane that has no turning. The client is warned of upsets along the road but the newspapers and magazine reader turns to his " horoscope " for reassurance and encouragement and infallibly he gets it. In the closing months of the 1930s the average citizen desperately wanted reassurance that there would be no war – and he received it in good measure. When war actually broke out, he wanted reassurance that it could not last long, that the enemy was far weaker than he appeared. To the strategists' stories of German tanks made of cardboard was now joined the astrologers' confident predictions that Adolf Hitler would die, go mad, be deposed or, in general, be rendered incapable of harming. The public lapped it up : shortage of paper alone prevented an astrological boom and by 1941 the cult had assumed such impressive proportions that Mass Observation added it to the significant social trends which it was analysing. Approximately forty per cent of the British people had some form of belief in the efficiency of astrology, the survey discovered.

The rise in belief in astrology was neatly matched by the decline in formal religious faith. But religious faith had been put to no such test as astrology had been by the unpredicted outbreak of war. How did astrologers explain this away and how accurate were their predictions now that each was subject to the gaze of millions? The magazine *Picture Post*, scenting the kind of sociological article in which it excelled, undertook its own investigations. They were of the simplest – and the most devastating to astrologers. All that was required was to pick out some of the more dramatic of the astrologers' predictions regarding the course of the war and see how they developed in fact and, conversely, to pick out some of the more obvious turning points of the war and check back to see if they had been predicted. The chances of success turned out to be almost wholly random, accuracy being produced at about the ratio of tossing a coin. R. H. Naylor undoubtedly made the most resounding error. The German invasion of Russia took place on Sunday, 22 June 1941 : on that same day Naylor's readers in the *Sunday Express* were firmly informed that there was not the slightest chance of Germany and Russia quarrelling in the near future. Nevertheless, out of the seven astrologers who were assessed in the article, Naylor came out the highest with a total of twelve points out of a possible thirty.

Five months later *Picture Post* returned to the attack. In the interim, the article had received wide publicity : scores of readers wrote in, the majority of them attacking the astrologers. Stung, the astrologers organised some kind of defence, the leading members of the fraternity attending a well-publicised lunch in London where each argued his or her case. They might, perhaps, have done well to have co-ordinated their speeches for they ranged from the defiant Old Guard who insisted that the stars actually controlled all mundane affairs to the hesitant modernists who would have their hearers believe that they were merely psychologists in fancy dress. The *Picture Post* article precipitated another avalanche of mocking letters and the editors of some of the popular newspapers involved quietly discontinued their astrological columns ' for the duration '. Even so, a sufficient number continued to practise and so gave rise to a question in the House when the Minister of Information was asked whether he would take steps to ban astrological predictions in the national interest. The Minister declined on the ground that no one took them seriously.

The Minister was not wholly accurate: a section of his own Government was, in fact, paying out good money to a certain Captain Louis de Wohl, journalist, novelist, refugee, and now Astrologer Extraordinary to HM Government. His presence on the British payroll was a remarkable exercise in the art of double bluff, for he had managed to convince a sufficient number of influential people that Hitler was employing an astrologer and it was therefore to the Allied interest to know precisely what that astrologer was predicting.

Astrology in Germany had been profoundly affected by the rise of the Nazi party. In the days immediately following the war and later through the Weimar Republic the craft had flourished, as it usually did in periods of great unrest and uncertainty. Side by side had grown up those occult societies and beliefs which have always had such a powerful hold on the Germanic mind so that, by the end of the 1920s, there existed in Germany as rich a stew of occultism as could be found anywhere in Europe.

The Nazi Party, once it had achieved power, set itself to purge the country. Nazism was not, of itself, incompatible with esoteric beliefs and occult practices: the extraordinary fantasies evolved by Heinrich Himmler bore testimony to that. Rather was it a repetition of the situation which had prevailed in Rome during the tyranny of the Emperors: it was very dangerous to predict bad luck for the ruling clique. A woman astrologer, Elsbeth Ebertin, had, in fact, brought off a remarkable prediction in 1923 when she had published a warning that Hitler should not undertake any important action in November. Disregarding the warning, he took part in the *Putsch* and ended up in Landsberg Prison.

Hitler's edict virtually put an end to astrology in Germany – until the Second World War was some three months old. A Swiss astrologer, Karl Ernest Krafft, who was living in

Germany in 1939, was privately asked by a member of the Government to prepare some astrological predictions. The request apparently emanated from Heinrich Himmler's department, a fact which could explain the rather dangerous ignoring of an edict from the Führer. Krafft replied with a warning that Hitler's life would be in danger in November 1939. In that month there occurred the Munich bomb plot when Hitler narrowly escaped assassination in a beer cellar. Krafft was promptly arrested, but was able to persuade his interrogators that his foreknowledge came from no more sinister a source than the stars in their courses. He was released and thereafter began to work for the Propaganda Ministry.

In his autobiography, *The Stars of War and Peace,* Louis de Wohl maintained that he learned of Krafft's activities through an indirect source. The Romanian Ambassador in London, who was in contact with Krafft, received from him a prediction of the future course of the war. It appeared to the Ambassador that Krafft was, willingly or not, working for the Nazis and it was the Ambassador who, making use of his high-level social connections, was able to recommend de Wohl for the job of counter-attacking Krafft. de Wohl's task was the classic case of hunting for a black cat in a coal cellar at midnight. He not only had to make his own findings coincide with those of Krafft's, but he also had to guess how much Krafft was likely to pass on to the Führer. Considering that, as Germany's position worsened, even the professional military advisers hesitated to give Hitler bad news, it seems unlikely that the astrologers would have passed on a tenth of what they discovered if it were inauspicious. Krafft, the person whom de Wohl believed he was combating, in any case disappeared from the scene very early in the war. He was sincerely dedicated to the craft of astrology and courageously, if foolishly, declined to be manipulated for propaganda purposes. He was packed off to a concentration camp as a result, where he died in 1944.

de Wohl's career contains most of the perplexing,

contradictory elements which abound in the personalities of professional astrologers. Much of the evidence in his auto-biographies can be discounted for they rather convey the impression of how Louis de Wohl and the stars together overcame the sinister might of Nazism. There is little doubt that he climbed on to a bandwagon which obligingly halted before him : he was, after all, faced with the problem of all refugees − how to make a living in a strange land. The majority of his predictions that can be checked are wholly inaccurate and those which were not are purely noncommittal. He was a highly intelligent man − his book on Thomas Aquinas was very well received − yet, despite his personal knowledge that his work in astrology was useless, he seemed capable of maintaining a sturdy and constant belief in his capabilities and in the craft he was serving. Self-delusion can operate independently of intelligence.

Meanwhile, in Germany, astrology was undergoing yet another suppression at the hands of the Nazis, following the flight of Rudolph Hess to Britain. Furious and embarrassed, seeking a scapegoat who could be accused of influencing Hess in his madness, Hitler ordered a thorough roundup of all astrologers in the Reich. He was probably on good grounds for thinking that Hess had been influenced by the stars, and the general suppression of astrologers was also justified, at least from the Party's point of view, on the grounds that their intensely individualistic work was at variance with the ethos of a totalitarian state. But, ironically, astrology was to provide a bizarre commentary on the last days of the Third Reich − and that in the very heart of Hitler's bunker. H. R. Trevor-Roper tells the story in his study of the dying struggles of the Reich − *The Last Days of Hitler*. On his return to the Propaganda Ministry on Friday, 13 April, Goebbels was greeted with the news that Roosevelt was dead. Overjoyed, Goebbels ordered champagne and immediately telephoned the Führer, who was then buried ten feet deep in his concrete bunker. ' My Führer, I congratulate you. Roosevelt is dead.

It is written in the stars that the second half of April will be the turning point for us. This is Friday, 13 April. It is the turning point.' Goebbels was referring to Hitler's horoscope which, despite the prohibitions on astrology, was not only allowed to exist but was kept in a secure place. Goebbels had no personal belief in astrology. 'Crazy times call for crazy measures' was his reply when asked why he had allowed its practitioners to continue. And despite the assurances of Louis de Wohl, Hitler, nihilistic rather than fatalistic, normally had not the slightest belief in the practice or theory. But cowering in his concrete grave with the booming of Russian guns only yards away, shattered in mental and physical health, there was every reason why he should grasp at this most illusory of straws. As Trevor-Roper remarks dryly: 'It is a pity that the science of astrology should have failed *all* its devotees.'

The predictive astrologer depends heavily – one might say exclusively – on two factors: the shortness and selectiveness of his client's memory and that client's reluctance to buy more than two or, at the most, three similar publications. The rare lucky shots are remembered: brought out in conversation they are inevitably embroidered. The vast number of inaccurate or simply irrelevant predictions are forgotten; there is, after all, no conversational value in a prediction that was not fulfilled. Similarly, the fact that most people buy, on average, no more than two newspapers a day or perhaps three magazines a week means that astrological predictions are very rarely compared. Within the context of astrological theory it would be unreasonable to expect an identity of phraseology in two or more predictions for the same person or event. The astrologer claims that while the mathematics for the erection of a horoscope must necessarily be constant, the interpretation can vary over a very wide range. Nevertheless, there should be a basic correspondence between two sets of interpretation. It would, for example, be reasonable for one interpretation to say that the client was going on a long journey, while another maintains that the journey would be short. But it would be wholly unacceptable for one interpretation to predict a journey and the other to predict that the client would remain at home. Comparison of a number of ' predictions ', however, shows that this contradiction happens as often as not.

The following seven horoscopes predicted events for the first week, or the whole of August 1971, for the same subject – the present writer. The first five are taken from women's magazines – the most fruitful in the field : the last two were taken from two, random, general newspapers.

1. 19 (Title of magazine). No author is named for the feature.
If born towards the end of the month be prepared for the first signs of readjustments due to take place in general spheres of your life. A change of job is one possibility which could happen fairly quickly. All Geminis should resist clinging to the old (and probably outworn) and try to cultivate the new and novel. Social life and romance will be happy. But watch a jealous friend! Good days 4th, 12th, 17th, 26th, 31st.

2. *Honey*. No author named for feature.
Geminians have been facing life with their usual happy-go-lucky though practical attitude but Saturn has been casting a rather dull shadow on things lately. At the same time he favours anything needing concentration and study – exams for instance. There's also a general enlivening glow from Venus on the 4th, a combination which brings a more serious attitude to a fairly frivolous love affair. Wednesdays are red letter days.

3. *Woman's Own*. Author : Leon Petulengro.
This week could bring you a new interest and perhaps some special news. Your artistic creativeness is given a chance to develop itself. Plenty of activity romantically for the single girl – a flirtation begun frivolously could be serious. Also an indication of a sudden attraction and whether you are free to be involved or not. Watch what you're doing : reckless indul-

gence could see you high and dry. Bring in your powers of persuasion and friendliness when it comes to organising something.

4. *Woman*. Author: Phyllis Naylor.
Changes are around you this week but they could affect relatives rather than yourself. *Your job*. You should do well in the first few days of the week. Later you may have to stand up for your rights. *Home and Marriage*. If single, you may put off the idea of getting married or engaged. If married you find you may have to make some changes at home. *Romance and social life*. Socially, you're in the limelight but you may not be in a romantic mood. There are practical problems to unravel.

5. *Woman's Realm*. Author: Katina Theodossiou.
Your partner comes up with some bright ideas which you support strongly. Family changes which have been brewing for some time come to a head.

6. *News of the World*. Author: Dorothy Adams.
Surprising news arrives this week but it could well be October before you notice the results. More travelling about. Lucky number 1.

7. *Evening Standard*. Author: Katina.
You may be feeling a little worried about a domestic situation this Saturday but your fears will be dispelled before the weekend is over. Do, however, make sure that you don't take on too much on behalf of relatives as you will find it more difficult to accommodate their needs or requests than you expect. Sunday very good for romantic dates, especially for lonely Geminians hoping to find the right partner.

On comparing the predictions the reader is struck not so much by the contradictions as by the sheer irrelevancies, one to another, of these predictions which are supposedly all intended for the same person. Running through all seven there is, admittedly, a sense of restlessness, of impending change but this is as much likely to arise from the fact that the horoscopes refer to August, traditionally a holiday month, as to any percipience on the astrologers' part. The style of most is vague and ambiguous enough but, even so, the contradictions stand out. Thus in No. 1, the client is urged to ' resist clinging to the old: cultivate the new and novel ', while in No. 2 it is stressed that this is the time for ' anything needing concentration and study – exams for instance '. In No. 1 again, the ' lucky days ' for the ensuing month are the 4th, 12th, 17th, 26th, 31st; in No. 2 lucky days are the Wednesdays. The Wednesdays in August 1971 occurred on 4th, 11th, 18th and 25th respectively – giving only one correspondence between the two supposedly identical lists. The shortness of Nos. 5 and 6 at least reduces the opportunity for error.

The seven forecasts do, however, have one important aspect in common : not one of the events predicted took place as far as the present writer was concerned – no romantic affair, no change of job, no surprising news, no domestic crisis. August was just another month.

Mundane astrology – the prediction of general world affairs rather than personal – once dominated in the popular press but is now wholly relegated to special magazines such as *Prediction, Horoscope* and *Old Moore's Almanac.* The publishers of this latter claim that it is the original edition ' dating back to 1697 ' and the *Almanac* certainly inherits the immense confidence of a much earlier generation of seers. Unlike the personal horoscopes in the periodical press with their carefully vague forecasts, the astrologers employed by *Old Moore's Almanac* give the most precise and minute details. It was predicted for October 1970, for instance, that ' The Government of China loses control of the country and the RAF will have to protect British interests in Asia '. In December 1970 ' The police will catch a gang of thieves specialising in the theft of meat from the docks '. Nothing is too small – ' New safety regulations about paraffin oil heaters ' – for consideration, or too large – ' Russian warships will provoke every type of incident at sea and will commit every possible act of aggression but will show themselves lacking the courage to take the final step to war.'

The year 1970 was, in general, predicted to be especially perilous at sea. This was because ' 1970 reduces to 17 and again to 8. The 17th letter in the Hebrew alphabet is Pe, and its planetary ruler is Mars: the 8th letter is Ceth, its ruler is Cancer – water.' International affairs are forgotten even quicker than personal affairs and it takes more than a casual act of memory to turn up the fact that there were no meat thefts in Britain in December; Mao Tse-tung did not lose control in China; the Russians were, if anything, unusually mild in their foreign relationships.

' 1970: World Predictions. What the Planets show for 1970 ' is the unequivocal title of a lengthy article in *Horoscope*. On closer inspection, however, there seems little in it that could not have been compiled by an intelligent observer of world affairs. Much play is made with technical jargon – ' transiting Saturn will be opposite the Soviet Union's natal Sun by mid-1970. This restrictive influence not only afflicts the luminary but also squares Russia's natal Neptune on one side and natal Uranus on the other ' – but little in the way of hard facts emerge. There is a warning to be ready for much racial troubles and student riots because of the passage of Neptune through Sagittarius even though it would require an optimism bordering on lunacy *not* to expect racial troubles and student riots in the present emotional climate. Similarly the information that ' Soviet diplomacy is both secret and ruthless ' seems merely a statement of rather self-evident fact than a glimpse into the future, as is the information that China is planning to develop nuclear weapons.

The bulk of *Horoscope* is concerned with personal forecasts which, as random tests show, despite their far greater length, achieve no greater degree of accuracy than the staccato predictions in popular periodicals. *Prediction* also leans heavily on personal forecasts with a similar degree of success, but in its articles extends into the wider world of the occult – ghost reports, manipulation of tarot cards, palmistry and the like. The implicit relationship between astrology and the occult is made explicit in all these specialist magazines by the advertisements. In the more sophisticated publications such as *Prediction,* the advertisements are, in the main, limited to announcements of the services of astrologers, spiritualist mediums and esoteric societies. Most are sober, although some seem to exist in defiance of the Trades Description Act with its pedantic insistence that the advertiser should provide that which he advertises.

> What would it be worth to you if you could utter one single word which would instantly cause any pain to vanish? Or to say another word – and immediately recover any lost or mislaid property? Or, with another word, invoke financial abundance and a flood of prosperity into your life?

By investing only 90p in a single book the most casual enquirer can gain access to 'magic words of power' which, among other affects, will 'make you immune to personal hazards, reveal secrets long hidden to you, help you find lost treasures, enable you to win at anything you attempt'.

But it is in the advertisement pages of *Old Moore's Almanac* that the reader gains a view into a world that has long since vanished from the pages of the popular press, a world which probably differs in no significant detail from any other period in previous history, for it is a world in which the future can be controlled by significant action in the present. The same advertisements appear year after year, arguing, at the least, that the advertisers receive sufficient return to make it worthwhile to repeat. Astrology here is merely another way of influencing 'luck' in theory. All that the astrologer can do is to say what will happen in the future – good or bad; in advertising practice the reader is assured that merely applying for a horoscope will bring good luck. 'Thousands of people have found that my predictions have been their turning point towards a better, brighter future – even though previously their lives seemed really black with no sign of hope or happiness on the horizon ', one such advertisement claims unequivocally. A rival backs up her claim with the offer of a four-leafed clover; another makes capital out of the fact that the vast majority of people have not the least idea of the time of their birth – without which an astrological prediction is meaningless even within its own context. Mixed in with the occult advertisements are others which give a clue to the readership of these pages, for they are directed at those suffering from some sense of personal inadequacy and counsel – how to avoid being bald, being a bore, improve memory, develop a beautiful bust, abolish acne. But it is the magical which dominates, in particular the offers to supply pixie charms which will infallibly change the course of life.

In theory, a full horoscope contains what is virtually an infinite number of factors – the total has been calculated at 539,370,750 plus thirty noughts. It makes therefore an ideal subject for the great twentieth century fashion of the computer and, given the equally strong interest in astrological predictions, a minor industry in ' computerised horoscopes ' came into being during the 1960s. One, based on an IBM 360/25 computer, was claimed to have been programmed with over nine million pieces of information and supplied seven pages of information. Unlike many human astrologers, its advertisements requested the birth time as well as the birth date and, if that could not be provided, based its calculation on a presumed birth date at 12 noon. A variation of this electronic astrologer was installed in Grand Central Station, New York, operating for a mere $5 fee. The amount of information programmed into the machine was impressive, for it took some ten minutes before the result was printed out on a continuous slip, forming some fifteen pages of information. But electronic astrologers shared the same wary approach to fatalism as their human fellows. ' The stars influence, but do not summarily dictate your future,' the print-out warned its reader. ' Man, having free-will, largely determines his own fate.' The threat of mass-produced, computerised horoscopes apparently paralysing the national will was taken sufficiently seriously in Britain for a Member of Parliament to seek a restriction on the sale of such products. But a random check of computerised horoscopes showed no significantly greater accuracy in its predictive qualities than that from fallible human beings. The large number of character analyses fed into the computer, combined with the lengthy nature of the print-out, did result in a number of apposite summaries of personalities – some of them of a startlingly exact nature.

I

Chapter 9
The Grammar of Astrology

A horoscope states simply that, at a certain point of time and relative to a certain point on the Earth's surface, the ten major members of the solar system were in certain positions in space. The Sun and the Earth's moon are treated as planets, but the moons of the other planets ignored. Apart from this fact the horoscope is something of which an astronomer could whole-heartedly approve. It is the interpretation of the chart which arouses the rage of the rational who deny that there is any-thing to interpret. It is also the interpretation which sparks off the bitterest controversy between astrologers themselves. There is no single authoritative method : there is no one authoritative meaning for any given symbol. Rather it is as though two or more people were to interpret an abstract painting or, more appropriately, an ink-blob test.

The erection of the horoscope proceeds along clearly defined mathematical lines. It is assumed that the Earth lies at the centre with the Sun moving around it, tracing an apparent path around the heavens known as the ecliptic. The ecliptic forms the spine of the Zodiac – that is, all planets, except Pluto, move along a narrow band traced in either side of the ecliptic. This band is divided into twelve sections, each with its sign. Because the Earth is itself rotating about its axis, each sign will appear to be moving from east to west.

The position of the Sun at birth is easy enough to determine

as most people know the exact date of their birth. Few, very
few, know the hour or, better still, the minute of birth and it
is only from knowledge of the time of birth that the astrologer
can calculate which sign of the Zodiac was in the ascendant –
i.e. rising above the eastern horizon at the moment of birth. It
is this ignoring of the time of birth that makes nonsense, even
within the astrological context, of the newspaper 'horoscopes'.
If they are erected by reasonably honest astrologers, they will
be based on the assumption that birth took place at noon – the
ultimate in hit or miss. Even if, by the law of averages, the
reader's birthtime was, indeed, at noon there is still another

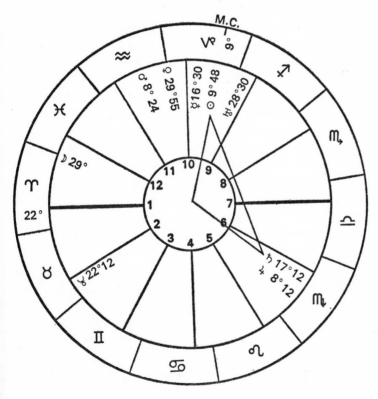

33 The horoscope for England as at Christmas Day 1066 – the
Coronation Day of William the Conqueror

elementary calculation missing – and that is the calculation based on his place of birth. There will obviously be a great difference in the ascendant at birth if the birth took place in Australia or Greenland. In theory it is possible for an astrologer to ' rectify ' a horoscope – that is, to arrive at a date/time/place of birth by calculating backwards from the events of the subject's life. What the astrologer is saying, in effect, is that because such and such an event has happened the subject must have been born at such and such a time, for only this combination of circumstances could have given rise to the later event.

Armed with the three vital pieces of information regarding date, time and place of birth, the astrologer begins by dividing his circular chart into four sections. Let it be assumed that he is erecting the horoscope of a person born at 1.36 p.m. on 21 March 1936, in London. The first division made is that by drawing the line connecting ascendant and descendant. Few, if any, modern astrologers make their own calculations and information is obtained from the published *ephemeris* and tables of houses. At 1.36 p.m. on the birthday Sagittarius was rising, the ascendant lying at 22° 6′. This is the first calculation to be entered. Next comes the vertical division made by the *medium coeli* or noon and *imum coeli* or midnight. A different sign of the Zodiac rises above the horizon every four minutes and progresses towards the highest point of the circle above the earth – the *medium coeli*. At noon on this particular day the sign at the *medium coeli* was 6° Scorpio. This is plotted, though the descending line connecting it with the lowest point – midnight – is not necessarily drawn. The positions of the houses, obtained from the published tables, are successively plotted, and then finally the positions of the planets are plotted. This completes the erection of the horoscope – but the interpretation has not even begun.

The interpretation of a horoscope is founded essentially upon the geometric relationships between all the symbols on

30 The newspaper astrologer R. H. Naylor, speaking in defence of astrologers at a luncheon in 1941

31 Louis de Wohl, temporary astrologer extraordinary to the wartime British Government

32 Delegates to the 1950 convention of the American Federation of Astrologers

the chart. Everything has a significance, even the space between the symbols – rich, exotic terminology, exists for every relationship but the meaning of the relationships are, to a very large extent, the personal contribution of the astrologer.

Over the centuries an immense corpus of information has been accumulated. Frequently – indeed, usually – the interpretations of one generation are dropped by the succeeding unless there is something unusually apposite or dramatic or distinctive about them. Astrological 'cookbooks' exist, classifying hundreds or even thousands of interpretations and putting them together is probably the extent of the average commercial astrologer's work. But even at the lowest, purely mechanical level there is an undeniable fascination in sorting through the scores of interpretations to create a unique combination that, hopefully, might yield some information on the subject. It is, perhaps, a kind of psychological Identikit in which fixed pieces are used to try and capture something that is, and must remain, eternally evanescent.

The following are the major elements in a horoscope. The largely technical elements forming the chart comes first and the planets at the end because the position on the chart profoundly modifies the 'meaning' of the planet. It must always be remembered that, while each element is vital to the whole, each is modified by its relationship to others.

THE HOUSES

These are the twelve divisions of the sky. Their position is exactly the same on all horoscopes – it is the Zodiac which moves.

Deciding where the exact boundaries – or cusps – of each house occur is an impossible task: certainly it has not yet been solved after centuries of calculations. As with so much else in astrology, the practitioner has had no choice but to close his eyes to the problem and choose a system which does not conflict too much with probability. The system chosen is usually that of Regiomontanus, the German forerunner of Copernicus.

1st house: Childhood, beginning: personal and physical appearance of the subject (the native) of the horoscope.

2nd house: Possessions in general, with particular emphasis on money.

3rd house: Transport and communication, including letters, speech, electronic communication. Relations in general, including neighbours and family.

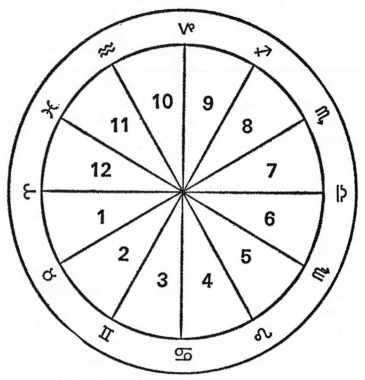

34 The Houses. These divisions are fixed in each horoscope: it is the outer ring, containing the signs of the Zodiac, which moves

4th house: The home of the native – but also his/her place of birth. Parents: buildings and, by extension, architecture.

5th house: Amusement, recreation and entertainment. Sex, children.

6th house: Health, work, food. Physical conditions in general.

7th house: Marriage: business partners and activities arising from business relationship.

8th house: Death and loss generally.

9th house: Travel, study, religion, philosophy. The church as an organisation. In general, movement, and the transmission of ideas.

10th house: The native's career: matters relating to his/her ambitions.

11th house: Social organisations and their effect upon the native.

12th house: Imprisonment, limitations, sorrow.

Each house is associated with a planet and a sign of the Zodiac: 1st: Aries, Mars. 2nd: Taurus, Venus. 3rd: Gemini, Mercury. 4th: Cancer, Moon. 5th: Leo, Sun. 6th: Virgo, Mercury. 7th: Libra, Venus. 8th: Scorpio, Mars. 9th: Sagittarius, Jupiter. 10th: Capricorn, Saturn. 11th: Aquarius, Saturn. 12th: Pisces, Jupiter.

The discovery of Uranus and Neptune enabled them to be substituted for Saturn and Jupiter in the 11th and 12th houses respectively. Most astrologers now adopt this relationship although purists insist on following the older system. The effect of the relationship is to increase the influence of any planet which is plotted in its 'own' house. Mercury in the Third House, for example, would signify an increase in intellectual activity – providing that there were no modifying factors.

THE ASPECTS

The aspects well demonstrate the fact that everything in a horoscope can be invested with significance, for they are simply the geometrical relationship of the planets with each other. In order to obtain the aspect, a line is drawn from the planet to the centre of the chart (the Earth).

Conjunction: O°

Negative – i.e. the effect is produced by the inter-relationship of the two planets' natures. In some cases, the effect of the inter-relationship will increase, in others decrease the ' natural ' tendency of the planet. For example Jupiter (law/harmony) in conjunction with Mercury (intellect/criticism) could produce a situation where intellectual ferment is slowly giving place to a maturity of judgement. On the other hand Jupiter in conjunction with Saturn could well be associated with a period of tyranny, as Saturn is credited with being an inward-looking, somewhat inhibited planet.

Opposition: 180°

In general, an indication of tension, disharmony, the tendency being for each planet to heighten the other's bad qualities, and eliminate the better influences.

Trine: 120°

An auspicious aspect, indicating that the planets involved are harmonious, working together towards a beneficial end.

Square: 90°

Another inauspicious aspect, a heightened version of the effect of *Opposition* – i.e. disharmonious, both planets either drawing out the worst in the other or cancelling out the better qualities.

Sextile: 60°
Favourable as trine. In trine, the tendency is towards physical
relationships, whereas sextile emphasises the intellectual or
non-tangible.

THE ZODIAC

This is the showpiece of the horoscope, the lynchpin of astrology – unfortunately suffering from one tremendous defect,
produced by that optimal slow rotation known under the grand
name of the ' precession of the equinoxes.' Astronomically, the
cause of this is a very slow change in the direction of the earth's
axis of rotation, causing the celestial poles to describe circles
among the stars, each circle taking 25,800 years to complete.
Astrologically, the effect is to displace each of the Signs:
some 2,000 years ago, for example, the spring equinox was in
Aries, today it is in Pisces and by the end of the century will
be in Aquarius. The reaction of the astrologers to this embarrassing fact of life was the traditional one – to pretend that it
did not exist. The stars in the sign known as Gemini, for
instance, are not the stars which are actually there, but the
stars which should be there if it were not for the irritating
precession of the equinoxes.

In addition to its potentiality, each Sign of the Zodiac has
four additional attributes or functions: It is ' ruled ' by a
particular planet: it is either positive or negative and fixed,
cardinal or mutable and it belongs to one of the four elements.
Thus the sign of Aries is ruled by Mars, is positive and cardinal and belongs to the element of fire.

Aries the Ram: 21 March to 20 April. Positive: Cardinal:
Fire. Ruled by Mars.
Traditionally, the leader of the year, by association Aries has
come to signify the thrusting, pioneering type of person.
The fiery element indicates creativeness – but creativeness
arising out of the ability and desire to manipulate people

rather than things or even ideas. Although it is always profoundly misleading to make anthropomorphical symbols of
the Zodiac – they seem, indeed, almost to be opposite to their
apparent meaning – in the case of Aries a comparison with
the thrusting, vital, aggressive nature of the ram is inescapable. One would expect to find here some great captain of
industry, or successful general. It comes as no surprise to find
that Bismark was an Arien – but so was Van Gogh. The
Arien needs somebody behind him to consolidate what his
industry and impetuousness has gained. Without that overshadowed, backing-up lieutenant, the Arien's very drive and
dynamism can destroy him.

Taurus the Bull: 21 April to 21 May. Negative: Fixed:
Earth. Ruled by Venus.
Stolidity, calmness, gentleness – these are the supposedly
dominant factors in the Taurean personality. Ruled by Venus
who, in this context, is not only sexuality but human kindness,
the Taurean is affectionate, thoughtful, homeloving. The
' fixed' and ' earthy' nature of the Sign implies that the
native is difficult to shift from a particular course. Strength,
rather than intelligence, is the keynote of the Taurean personality – although this can be greatly modified if the
' intellectual' planet Mercury is also found in the Sign.

Altogether, the Taurean may reasonably be supposed to be
a good citizen, a loving husband and father. It just so happens
however that Adolf Hitler was a Taurean – a fact which
should give pause to anyone hoping to make a science out of
astrology. And if Adolf Hitler may be said to be an extreme
example, so too must be William Shakespeare, Yehudi
Menuhin and George Washington, all of whom were born
with the Sun in Taurus.

Gemini the Twins: 21 May to 21 June. Positive: Mutable:
Air. Ruled by Mercury.
Mercury was not only the divine postman, but also the patron

of thieves and the dichotomy is faithfully reflected in the Geminian character. The mutable, airy, positive attributes of Gemini indicates the restless, inquisitive, imaginative personality of the native. At its most auspicious, the horoscope of the Geminian is that of an intellectual, a person fond of juggling with words, enamoured of novelty and experiment – attributes which perhaps can be recognised in John F. Kennedy and Jean-Paul Sartre. Intuition plays a larger part in the mental process than laborious deduction. The reverse of these virtues is fickleness, a dislike of routine, a febrile shallowness. In an extreme form, these weaknesses can degenerate into actual lunacy. The dual form of the sign makes it the appropriate astrological guardian of the lungs with their two-way action.

Cancer the Crab: 22 June to 22 July. Negative: Cardinal: Water. Ruled by the Moon.
This sign is the ideal demonstration of the fact that the symbols of the Zodiac owe their origin to some other cause than anthropomorphism. The crab, in nature, could reasonably be taken for the symbol of either a grasping, vicious personality or of emotional coldness at best for there is, after all, little overtly loving about a crab's personality. In the Zodiac pantheon, however, it stands for mother-love, among other improbable attributes.

In the anti-clockwise cycle of the horoscope, Cancer is the first of the 'water' signs: it is also Cardinal – and ruled by the Moon. The association between the Moon and women is obvious: a further extrapolation brings in the concept of the ocean as the mother of all things. Cancer can therefore simultaneously stand for profundity in thought or emotion and also for the home – with particular emphasis on childhood. Associated with these 'soft-centred' ideas is the concept of the crab's carapace, the whole combining to make up a personality which is tough and uncompromising externally, but internally is highly sensitive and artistic. Such a character may – or may not – bear affinity to Julius Caesar, for example, born with the Sun in Cancer, or with Rembrandt.

Leo the Lion: 23 July to 23 August. Positive: Fixed: Fire. Ruled by the Sun.

The Lion ruled by the Sun – and, moreover, a fixed, fiery, positive symbol. Such a combination of circumstances can add up only to the most auspicious of signs, associated with leadership and success. The inherent contradiction between its fiery and fixed nature can perhaps be resolved by postulating that where the fire indicates energy and creativeness, the fixity indicates a central core of resolve. At its most auspicious, therefore, the horoscope of the Leonian indicates a strong-minded, highly-intelligent person who knows where he is going and intends to get there with the least possible delay. It is the horoscope of the revolutionary as well as the established king, including Mussolini as well as Louis XIV – the Sun King. The reverse features of the sign are suspicion and arrogance.

Virgo the Virgin: 24 August to 23 September. Negative: Mutable: Earth. Ruled by Mercury.

This is one of the Signs which has changed its appearance during recorded history. Originally, Virgo was a young girl: today she tends to be an older woman and the interpretation has therefore subtly changed to indicate excellent, but somewhat old-maidish, qualities, as opposed to the earlier concept of youth and the qualities arising from it. The change is interesting, not least because it was never made by the edict of some central authority but a blind response to a popular feeling.

The Sign is usually shown holding a sheaf – presumably of wheat – and links Virgo back to the ancient tradition of Ceres. But the fact that the sign is ruled by the intellectual Mercury introduces a leaven in what could be a somewhat heavy combination of housewifely virtues. Virgo is at once mutable and earthy, indicating a readiness to contemplate new ideas but also an ability to conserve that which is valuable. Cardinal Richelieu and Greta Garbo presumably share affinities for both are Virgo.

Libra the Scales: 24 September to 23 October. Positive: Cardinal: Air. Ruled by Venus.
The only non-living sign. Libra shares the same ruler as Taurus and therefore has something of the Taurean qualities of gentleness and affection. It is the sign of the autumn equinox and therefore exactly opposite that of Aries, the spring equinox. Extrapolating from the normal meaning of the sign, later astrologers have given the Libran native the qualities of balance and of justice, arguing from thence that the Libran will make a good negotiator or diplomat – qualities that characterise at least two Librans – Mahatma Gandhi and Pope Paul VI.

Scorpio the Scorpion: 24 October to 22 November. Negative: Fixed: Water. Ruled by Mars.
Anthropomorphism totally dominates this sign for it is assumed that the qualities of the scorpion are also the qualities of the native. It so happens that the Sign is also associated with the 8th House, traditionally the house of death. The sinister tendencies are further reinforced by the fact that many astrologers assign the newly-discovered planet Pluto, in place of Mars, as ruler of the Sign.

No one Sign is wholly good or wholly bad however and the virtues of Scorpio are its vices reversed. The Scorpionic character is, if anything, even more prone to schizophrenia than the Geminian. Mars rules it and Mars can indicate either great strength or great cruelty: it is watery and fixed, indicating the possibilities of great depth of character. In sum, the Scorpionic native could either be a person of immense willpower and ambition, sensitive but forceful, or a person delighting in his power over others and using that power sadistically. All astrologers agree in crediting the Scorpionic native with great sensuality, which can amount to eroticism. It is perhaps not surprising to find Martin Luther and Mata Hari both under the sign of Scorpio.

Sagittarius the Archer: 23 November to 21 December. Positive: Mutable: Fire. Ruled by Jupiter.
This is another Sign which has changed over the centuries. Originally, Sagittarius was always shown as a centaur; today, although the centaur image still persists, it is as often shown simply as an archer. The symbol does not help, for it is merely that of an arrow and whether or not the centaur image originally held any greater significance than the concept of the dart or arrow cannot now be determined. The more occult type of astrologer will insist on maintaining the centaur for it fits in neatly enough with the concept of human and animal passions/attributes warring for dominance.

The key to this Sign is its ruler, Jupiter – the king of the gods. The Sagittarian expects to lead, to dominate. But one of Jupiter's characteristics is a somewhat boisterous good fellowship – ' joviality ' – which will help to temper the naked will to power. The concept of the archer, whether as human or centaur, is extended into the native's personality not as a warrior but a huntsman and thence, by extrapolation, as a person who delights in outdoor sports and activities. In general, one would expect a Sagittarian to be a big, bluff, rather noisy and jolly fellow with nevertheless a shrewd eye to the main chance and – since his is a fiery sign – considerable ability to create or initiate. Winston Churchill was born under Sagittarius; so also was General de Gaulle – and the resulting conflict between them would have been precisely what an astrologer would expect.

Capricorn: 22 December to 20 January. Negative: Cardinal: Earth. Ruled by Saturn.
Capricorn is the third Sign to have changed over the centuries.

Originally, it was pure monster – a goat with a fish's tail; today it is shown, as often as not, as an ordinary goat, losing something both of its decorative nature and its symbolism as a result.

This sign rules the dead period of the year. Admittedly, this applies only to the northern hemisphere but astrologers who can swallow the camel of a geocentric universe are not going to strain at the gnat of a northern-oriented system. Capricorn therefore reflects the qualities of winter and, ruled by the harsh, cold planet Saturn, is precisely the sign under which one would expect Joseph Stalin to be born – although it is as well to remember that it was also in the ascendant at the birth of Joan of Arc. The Capricornian is an excellent organiser, a disciplinarian if necessary, with a profound respect for authority. This is an earthy sign so the strength of the native does not lie in creating but rather in developing what others have commenced. There is a tendency to thrift which can, under some circumstances, turn to miserliness. Altogether, it would seem that the Capricornian would be an excellent member of society in the capacity of a lieutenant. An outstanding Capricornian, however, was the Emperor Augustus. In his day the fish-tailed goat ruled the Sign unchallenged whence the astrologer could argue that this sign, incorporating creatures at home in two elements, was the natural sign for a world ruler.

Aquarius the Water Carrier: 21 January to 19 February. Positive: Fixed: Earth. Ruled by Saturn and, later, Uranus. Owing to the precession of the equinoxes, the spring equinox will be occurring in Aquarius after having been occurring in the constellation of Pisces for the past 2,000 years. This is the dawning of the Age of Aquarius which most astrologers welcome as a period of peace and prosperity after two millennia of strife and chaos.

Aquarius is, essentially, the Sign of innovation and invention. The water which the Carrier pours out so generously is an indication of the benefits to be gained from science – a tendency emphasised by modern astrologers who prefer to substitute newly-discovered Uranus, the tutelary planet of Science, for old Saturn. The Sign, being both fixed and airy as well as positive, denotes a native who has the capacity for thought as well as the ability to apply what he has discovered. The Aquarian is a philanthropist in the widest possible sense – that is, while he rarely makes close friendships, he nurses a respect for humanity in the abstract. The ideal Aquarian, therefore, would be a scientist engaged in some study which would benefit mankind – probably medicine – and who had a tendency to display irreverence towards established institutions. Too cerebral – too intelligent, perhaps, to be an active revolutionary, the Aquarian could nevertheless be depended upon to support to the end any cause which took his approval. Charles Dickens is an excellent example of the Aquarian: so is Abraham Lincoln.

Pisces the Fishes: 20 February to 20 March. Negative: Mutable: Water. Ruled by Jupiter and Neptune.
Paradoxically the most violent of the Signs, signified by the Fish swimming against each other, and the weakest, being at once negative, mutable and watery. Traditionally, this is the sign of the Christian Era, ushered in by the precession of the equinoxes at about the time of Christ, and now on its way out.

At the individual level, the Sign frequently denotes the dreamer, the poet, the artist – all occupations under the control of Neptune, the magician and the dreamer. The imprecise nature of their Sign can imply either that they are diffident and uncertain to the point of negativeness, or that they are highly subtle and sensitive. They are supposed to be particularly susceptible to alcohol as a means of escaping the unrelenting pressures of life. On the credit side is the Piscean gentleness and intelligence, civilised qualities which makes them welcome to the discerning. Albert Einstein seems a good Piscean, Pius XII somewhat less so.

If the Houses and the Aspects are the stage, and the Signs the furniture and decorations, then the Planets are undoubtedly the actors in the astrological drama. The signs of the Zodiac are exotic and colourful but they leave no impress of personality: it is impossible to believe in the objective reality of a scorpion or a pair of fishes. It seems, however, only too easy to accept the objective reality of the personality of Mercury or Mars or any other of the family of god-planets, judging by the anthropomorphic qualities granted them by the prose of many an astrologer. But even those who remain indifferent to, or actively reject, the theories of astrologers are constrained to grant at least some attributes to the Planets if only because most of them are visible entities which, in the case of the Sun and the Moon, actively affect terrestrial environment. The names bestowed upon them, too, are heavy with history and legend: even the totally illiterate are aware of the attributes of the classical Mars and Venus, at least, and to invest the Planet with the attributes of the god does not necessarily require an active belief in paganism.

The Sun
This is the strongest of all the planets, so much so that, in popular mass-produced astrology its position is the only element in the horoscope. The native is as likely to be affected by Mercury or the Moon or Mars in some particular sign of the Zodiac but it is the position of the Sun-sign alone that is recognised. The sun is, inevitably, the male principal, the generative force – in general, the positive, intellectual element in nature. Its position in a woman's horoscope will be associated with her menfolk; in a man's horoscope it will indicate something about his career, his path through life. A well-aspected Sun indicates a native who is positive, forceful, successful and a natural leader; a badly aspected Sun does not

K

necessarily mean the opposite of these qualities but their degeneration. A native with such a Sun can be weak – but also he can be stupidly arrogant and intolerant. As with all the planets, its significance is modified by its associates. Thus the Sun in good aspect with Mercury implies a skill in speech and writing : in good aspect with Neptune argues the possession of intuition of a high order. Its relationship with its twin, the Moon, is regarded as being the most vital. Thus, when the two are in good aspect with each other, the horoscope refers to a balanced person who is at peace with himself and the world : in bad aspect, then he can expect an inharmonious, discordant period with unfortunate love affairs thrown in.

Each of the Planets is supposed to rule certain hours and days. The Sun's day is, naturally, Sunday, but its influence is particularly heightened at the 1st, 8th, 15th and 22nd hours.

The Moon

The Germans, with Teutonic perverseness, have made the Moon linguistically male : so did the Babylonians. But all other races associate the ethereal beauty of its light and its changefulness with femininity. In many ways it is difficult clearly to distinguish between the female influences of the Moon and the influences of Venus. In general, however, although both have an influence on the relationship between men and women, the influences of Venus tends to be overtly sensual while the Moon presides over a more spiritual love, as well as a non-sensual relationship between the sexes as, for example, between a man and his mother and daughters. The fastest moving of all the planets, completing thirteen orbits a year around the Earth as compared, say, with Mars' half an orbit, the Moon naturally is the genius of change and motion. It needs no occult interpretations to connect the Moon with water, and it therefore affects all those who go to sea or in any way derive their living from water – including members of the animal kingdom. In astrological medicine it is supposed to control the left eye and the digestive organs. At the individual level, the Luna native will probably be restless, intelligent and prone to act on impulse.

Mercury

The key to Mercury is the adjective ' mercurial ' defined by the Oxford English Dictionary as being ' sprightly, ready-witted, volatile '. Traditionally the youthful messenger of the gods, Mercury's attributes are those of thought and youth and, above all, changeability. Mercurians are supposed to share the same qualities of the metal mercury or quicksilver. The metal takes colour from its background : so does the native. The metal responds immediately to changes in temperature : the native also responds to changes in emotional temper. ' Mercury is lord of speech, as the Sun is lord of light. Whosoever is born under Mercury shall be subtle of wit and very crafty in many sciences. He shall love well to preach and to speak fair rhetoric language and to talk of philosophy and geometry.'

Mercury, in short, is the planet of the intellectual – but of the dashing, intuitive kind of mind which treats intellectual problems as games. In the absence of any compensating influences, the Mercurian can be shallow, fickle and downright criminal – the god was also the patron of thieves, after all. In morally neutral areas the planet indicates the capacity for speech, memory and writing : badly aspected, Mercury indicates that the native will be deficient in these qualities – perhaps suffering from a speech impediment or inability to read. The planet controls trade and, in modern interpretations, electronic systems of communication. Its day is Wednesday, the affinity being clearer in romance languages, mercoledi, mercredi.

Venus

The Venus symbol has been variously identified as being a looking glass, or the union of earth (+) and spirit (o). With the

35 The influence of Venus

symbol for Mars it has had a renewed life in modern zoology
where the two indicate that an animal is male or female.

The dominant attribute of Venus is, inescapably, love.
Venus in a favourable aspect portends beauty, elegance,
comfort for the native; badly aspected it implies an unfortunate love life – hence, an indication of loneliness. The
Venusian character is, perhaps, a hedonist – but an elegant
hedonist and one who would prefer to be amiable if it does
not require too great an expenditure of energy. Venus in good
aspect – particularly in conjunction with the Moon – indicates
a situation with a feminine bias or one which is dominated by
females. In non-personal, neutral situations such an aspecting
would merely refer to a predominately feminine profession or
occupation. In a personal, male horoscope, it would imply
that the man was unduly under the sway of his womenfolk,
or, alternatively, had much of the feminine about him. Zoo-
logically, Venus rules those birds and animals traditionally

36 Fifteenth-century French illumination, showing the
relationship of the seven planets to the twelve signs of the Zodiac
—e.g. Mars in armour is joined to Aries and Scorpio. Earth is in
the centre

37 An elaborate fifteenth-century German representation of the professions controlled, and the influences exerted by a particular planet. Saturn (shown here as a horseman, flanked by his signs of Capricorn and Aquarius) is almost entirely malignant, responsible for disease, misfortune and death—hence the gallows, stocks and the cripple. The professions shown are the farmer, the gardener and the tanner (Skinning a horse)

associated with the cult of the love goddess – doves, kingfishers, fauns. The planet's day is Friday – vendredi.

Mars

Mars and Venus have the greatest mutual effect on each other – undoubtedly a derivative result of the Ares-Aphrodite story as recorded by Homer. In good aspect to each other then they will produce a sensitive but firm, intelligent personality which is fully aware of the value of sensuous impressions but contains them within an ordered framework. A graphic artist would reasonably be expected to have his Mars and Venus in conjunction. Badly aspected then the native would be burdened with undue sexuality.

Mars is classed by the traditional astrologers as a malefic, contributing more than its proportion of evil and sorrow and yet necessary in the overall scheme of the horoscope even as sour as required as a complement to sweet in a menu, or a discordance to a harmonic in a piece of music. In neutral situations, Mars stands simply for power or force: well-aspected, that power will give strength to a planet or sign that lacks it. Badly aspected, then the power becomes brutality. He is a warrior, naturally influencing battles and quarrels but also, by extension, presiding over all those who use cutting instruments in their trade such as barbers and butchers. In reading a horoscope with a badly aspected Mars, care must be taken to decide whether such an effect is to make of the native a bully or the exact opposite, a coward. In either case, the planet's relationship with other planets, or the position on the horoscope will probably ameliorate the starkly bad qualities.

Jupiter

Jupiter is, above all others, a benefic planet. The personality with which the planet is endowed is not the over-sexed, frequently violent and tyrannous King of the Gods but rather a benevolent, patriarchal father-figure. He is the judge,

38 Scorpio, Taurus, Jupiter and (right) Saturn: a symbol of
disaster

guardian of the helpless, the consoler. It is Jupiter who gives
the ability and courage to carry on just that little further and
longer when everything seems hopeless. Well-aspected in a
personal horoscope, Jupiter portends material good fortune
for the native. Jovians are, in addition to being ' jovial ',
deeply moral, with a strong feeling for the sanctity of authority
and often religious. Badly aspected, the native can be boastful
and extravagant with a strong tendency to believe that the
world owes him a living. The animals he rules are such as the
elephant and other ' generous beasts of most descriptions '.

Saturn

The ascribing of a cold, sullen personality to Saturn is a good
example of reading into the personality of a planet qualities

derived from its physical place in the solar system. Until the discovery of Uranus in 1781, Saturn was the last and furthest out of all the planets, an object moving so slowly through dark, cold space that it took years to pass through one sign of the Zodiac. It was invested with the properties of night and old age – the 'saturnine' temperament, a combination of melancholy, suspicion and emotional coldness.

Nevertheless, as with his fellow planets, Saturn is good or bad in a personal horoscope in relationship to other factors. A badly aspected Saturn expresses clearly what is implied in the planet's personality – bad luck, miserliness, suspicion. One feels that it was a Saturnian who made the more lack-lustre of the proverbs ' Look before you leap ', ' A bird in the hand is worth two in the bush ' and the like. The Saturnian instinctively looks a gift horse in the mouth and would be pleased at finding his suspicions confirmed, if he ever showed pleasure. But this is a badly aspected relationship. In a more auspicious horoscope, Saturn will bestow some of the virtues of old age – sobriety, wisdom, discretion. Two Saturnians who dramatically show up this contrast are Joseph Stalin – preeminently the Saturnian in its bad aspect – and Albert Einstein.

Uranus

Uranus was the first of the planets whose discovery upset the delicate balance of the astrologers' universe. Discovered at the close of the eighteenth century, it was over a hundred years before its attributes were finally decided upon. Like its fellows Neptune and Pluto, it takes so very long to complete the circle of the Zodiac that astrologers agree that its influence must be taken as falling upon complete generations and not merely a single lifespan. Arguing backwards, astrologers ascribe to it those inventions which have taken place since its discovery – the more bolder will claim, in other words, that it was the discovery of Uranus that ushered in our modern technological society. Curiously, while ascribing the newest of inventions to

Uranus, one of the oldest of professions is placed under its tutelage and astrologers now proclaim themselves as the children of Uranus.

Despite the tacit agreement among more serious-minded astrologers that this slow-moving planet can have little effect upon individuals, astrological ' cookbooks ' obediently ascribed to it the most detailed of effects. In general, the tendency is to regard Uranus as the patron of eccentricity and rebellion, with many of the attributes, indeed, of Mercury.

Neptune

It is interesting to speculate what would have been the effect on astrology if the three newly-discovered planets had been given numbers or, at least, non-classical names as very nearly happened with Uranus. The current attributes of all three planets are certainly influenced by the knowledge of the roles of the classical gods who bore the same name. Thus, ultra-modern astrologers have awarded Neptune the governorship of the seas, in place of the Moon and, in addition, of all liquids – including such modern liquids as petrol. Tentatively, it is associated with magic and, in a bad aspect, with a grotesque distortion of reality. The fact that it takes nearly fifteen years to pass through a single Sign of the Zodiac means that, even in the astrological context, its influence on individuals is severely limited. Nevertheless, the more determined astrologers have wrung some sort of personal interpretation out of its movement, claiming that Neptune in a bad aspect is responsible for an obsession with drugs, hypnotism and a general desire to escape reality while, in a good aspect, he controls the visionary and the reformer.

Pluto

Pluto takes 248 years to complete a journey around the Sun and is quite invisible to the naked eye. These two factors alone tempted astrologers to ignore it when it was discovered in 1930. But to argue that a planet could have an effect upon human life only when its rays could be seen by the human eye placed the whole concept of planetary and stellar influence in jeopardy. Reluctantly, most astrologers have accepted it and there is a general consensus of opinion regarding its supposed attributes. These attributes, however, are so obviously produced by the name that it leaves the layman in doubt as to precisely who is controlling whom. Mythologically, Pluto is the god of the underworld and of death: hence the planet is the planet of destruction responsible, above all, for the discovery of the atomic bomb. Determinedly optimistic astrologers see in his destructive attributes the seed of future growth in the sense that it is necessary to demolish before construction can start.

39 Sixteenth-century illustration of the arrangement of the heavenly spheres

Chapter 10
The Books of the Prophets

Astrology is the queen of the predictive arts, presenting to the devotee, the sceptic and the layman alike an appearance of elegance and attraction. Visually, the symbols are capable of being combined and re-combined into an immense number of allegorical pictures which can be – and have been – used by such diverse groups as fifteenth-century alchemists and twentieth-century advertisers. Interpretatively, there are so many elements – some static but many moving – that their permutations allow an infinite number of combinations. The permutations can be adapted to virtually any character – or used as a neat way out if the predictions fail to come true. Scientifically, the planets may be dead lumps of matter or balls of gas; astrologically, they are living entities endowed with highly individual personalities.

Apart from aesthetics, astrology possesses one great virtue over all its rival systems: any given horoscope can be re-calculated by an independent observer after the event which it is supposed to have foretold and some sort of check levied upon its accuracy. Only too often, the famous prophecies of history turn out to have been uttered or written some time after the event. The notorious Mother Shipton is high in this class. She died in 1561 – but the first printed version of her prophecies did not appear till 1641. They proved, unsurprisingly, to be highly accurate for the late sixteenth and early seventeenth centuries but progressively less so thereafter.

Nevertheless, among the floods of highly dubious printed prophecies there does exist a handful of works which by reason of their provenance lay some claim to prophetic accuracy. In some cases it can be established that the prophecy was indeed in print or manuscript before the predicted event. More commonly, they owe their value to the fact that they were, as it were, continuously predicting – in other words, their prophecies refer to the recent past, the present and the near future as well as to remote antiquity and futurity and can therefore be subjected to a reasonably full degree of checking. Pre-eminent among these prophecies are the enigmatic *Centuries* of Nostradamus.

Nostradamus was born, in 1503, in St Rémy, the son of Christianised Jewish parents. He himself was baptised Michel and his parents probably took their name from the Notre Dame quarter in which they lived. His father was a physician and Michel, after studying law at Avignon, went on to Montpellier to study medicine. He was a hard-working, clever, but not particularly outstanding student. Nevertheless, within a few months of qualifying as a physician he made his mark throughout Provence. The plague struck Montpellier and for four years raged throughout the south. From the beginning, Nostradamus was unusually successful in his treatment. He seems to have invented or adapted some form of disinfectant which at once contributed to his confidence in treating the sick and may well have reduced the possibility of infection in any given household. Certainly his services were sought after, though there was some muttering among his fellow physicians who disapproved of his unorthodox medicines and treatment – medicines and treatment which seemed to work. Following the plague from town to town gave him a taste for wandering and, after the epidemic had abated, he continued to travel, remaining still in France but journeying ever further afield – yet another aberration in a period when people travelled only for the most pressing reasons. He married and knew a brief period of settled domestic happiness but, ironically, the skill which he had employed in the service of strangers was not sufficient to protect those he loved. The plague swept down again and his wife and two tiny children were carried off. Again he set off on his wanderings, this time going beyond the confines of France into Italy and as far as Sicily. Over a period of eight years the freemasonry of his profession opened doors to him wherever he found himself, enabling him not only to make a living but to study ever deeper in areas labelled ' Forbidden ' by the Church. He was, supposedly, a Christian and throughout his life prudently gave the impression of being a sincere convert. But his natural contacts in foreign cities tended to be the members of his own race and, through them, those Islamic scholars who had kept the sciences alive during their long sleep in the West.

It was in Italy that his curious faculty was first manifested. Later, the man's own writings were to act as permanent and unimpeachable testimony of his gift, but for this earlier period, when he was still essentially a wandering savant, posterity is dependent on what might be the constructions of hindsight, in particular legends created or innocently repeated by his disciples and biographers. *La Testament de Michel Nostradamus,* written by his pupil Chavigny, contains most of these stories, written in a sober manner, which, if it does not compel belief in the stories themselves, compels belief in the writer's integrity. Undoubtedly the most famous of these legends – or events – concerned the young monk Felix Peretti. Nostradamus encountered him on the road near Ancona – and promptly fell on his knees before him. The young man was as surprised as the spectators and dismissed Nostradamus' salutation ' I kneel before His Holiness ' as the babblings of a deluded mind. Thirty years later, however, Felix Peretti ascended the papal throne as Sixtus IV. Rather more circumstantial was the story of the sceptical farmer who asked Nostradamus to predict the fate of two sucking pigs in the farmyard. The black pig would be eaten for supper that night and a wolf would eat the white one, Nostradamus replied casually. The farmer promptly ordered his cook to kill and prepare the white pig for supper. This was done and during the meal Nostradamus was mocked for the failure of his prophecy. Unperturbed, he insisted that they were, in fact, eating the black pig, the white pig having been carried off by a wolf precisely as he predicted. The cook was summoned to the table and there confessed that he had, in fact, killed the white pig as ordered and prepared it for roasting but it had been seized by a young wolf cub which some of the farmer's men were attempting to tame. By the time he had driven the animal off there was little left to cook and he had therefore killed and prepared the second of the two pigs – the black pig.

These and many similar tales began to be told of the man, investing his name with a special aura, long before he had published a line of work. In retrospect, he seems to have been uncommonly fortunate in escaping the imputations of witchcraft: by the 1540s the hatred and fear of witches were at their irrational height. It was, perhaps, his success and devotion as a physician which protected him in the early days: an envious colleague did indeed accuse him of employing magic, but no one was anxious to deprive the community of an outstanding doctor during a period of regular recurrences of plague. And, later, he was to have the protection of the royal family.

In 1544 he was back again in France and in 1547 he settled finally in Salon, a small town some thirty miles from Avignon. He married a widow of substance, established himself as the leading physician of the town and now, comfortably off, turned to the written work that was to make his name virtually synonymous with prophecy. On 4 May 1555, the first edition of his *Centuries* was printed, in Lyons, by a certain Mace Bonhomme. The bibliographical detail is of some importance for while many of the enigmatic prophecies referred to events dizzy centuries distant, many, too, related to near-contemporary events and it is therefore possible to establish the sequence of development from prophecy to fulfilment, together with the judgement of contemporaries.

The first reaction of a modern reader of the *Centuries* is, usually, a mixture of total bewilderment and disappointment. The most famous book of prophecies in Western Europe turns out to be, on closer inspection, without discernible order, couched in language so obscure as to be capable of almost any meaning – where its meaning is not altogether impenetrable. The 'centuries' of the title have nothing to do with chronology : it has merely happened that the author has arranged his four-line verses in sections of one hundred verses. There is no apparent motive for placing a verse in one 'century' rather than another, for no 'century' has any discernible characteristic. Sometimes two or three verses dealing with the same subject succeed each other; in other cases, the related verses are scattered at random through the centuries.

But the eccentricity of the presentation is as nothing compared with the eccentricity of the language. The twentieth century reader is faced, at the outset, with the hazard of the literary conceit which was not merely acceptable but virtually obligatory for the writer of Nostradamus' period. Devices such as the pun and anagram, which have long since been purged from serious literature, are freely used and to them Nostradamus adds his own personal dimension of confusion. He transliterates from the Greek or Hebrew to the French and then puns or makes an anagram of the result; initials or abbreviations are employed quite arbitrarily; he invents his own nicknames for historical personages.

In his preface to the first edition of the *Centuries* Nostradamus claimed that the obscurity was deliberate.

> Although I have often foretold, long in advance, what had afterwards come to pass, acknowledging all to have been done by divine virtue and inspiration, I was willing to hold my peace by reason of the injury – not only of the present

time but also of the future – because to put them in writing would arouse the fury of the Kingdoms, Sects and Religions who might be diametrically opposed to them. For this reason I have withheld my tongue from the vulgar and my pen from paper. But afterwards I was willing, for the common good, to enlarge myself in dark and abstruse sentences, declaring the future event – chiefly the most urgent and those which I foresaw would not offend the hearers.

In this preface, and in a dedicatory letter to the King, Henri II, he outlined the course of his book and, with it, the course of all human affairs, employing his own chronology to do so. He pronounces upon the remote, antediluvian past as confidently as upon the remote future but the modern reader learns with considerable astonishment that Adam was created 1242 years before Noah, that Abraham followed Noah ' about a thousand and four score years afterwards ' and that between the creation of the world and Nostradamus' own date of writing – 1557 – a period of ' about 4,173 years and eight months more or less ' had elapsed. The history of the world is projected forward to the year 3797 but though there is a wealth of astrological and astronomical data from which it is just possible to erect a chronology, he gives only one hard date. This is 1792, ' a year that shall see a greater persecution against the Christian Church than ever was in Africa at which time everyone will think it an innovation of the age '. The French Revolution broke out in 1792 and it would seem that Nostradamus had scored a bull's-eye – were it not for the fact that, in the same paragraph he predicts the rise of Venice to a stature equal that of ancient Rome. In his letter to the King he stated unequivocally that ' I could have set down in every quatrain the exact time in which they shall happen but it would not please everybody '. Elsewhere, he hints that far greater and darker and more terrible secrets than those he is now publishing had come before his eyes.

I have seen many volumes which have been hidden for centuries. But dreading what might happen in the future, I presented them to Vulcan after having read them and as the fire began to devour them the flames, licking the air, created a brilliance as of lightning, shining all over the house as though it had been aflame.

Altogether, Nostradamus' prose introductions are the least impressive part of his work. The usual claim to dark secrets not permitted to lesser mortals; the tortuousness and obscurity of the language where clarity is not merely expected but necessary; the gross and detectable errors in the chronology of the past – all combine to give an effect of cloudy self-delusion. The effect of the quatrains themselves is far otherwise. The reader who has managed to struggle through a representative number of them finds, in fact, their very chaos and obscurity to be weirdly compelling for it is rather as though the writer were under the influence of a drug when words and associations come welling up from some literally occult source. Nostradamus gives only the most casual references to his method of work. Despite his free use of astrological terms, it is evident that his predictions are not based on the casting of horoscopes: the time factor alone would make such a method unlikely. In the second quatrain of the first *Century* he gives a tantalisingly oblique description of one of his prophetic sessions:

> With wand in hand, placed in the middle of the branches,
> I wet the limb and foot.
> A fearsome awe makes my hand tremble.
> Divine Splendour: the Divinity is seated nearby.

It is just possible to understand the description by relating it to the fairly common technique of divination by water. In this system a brass bowl, marked off in sections, is filled with water. The operator holds a divining rod over the water and at a certain moment of trance the rod will dip towards one or other of the sections, each of which has a particular significance. The probability is that, where the apparatus is not operated by an outright charlatan, it acts as a focusing medium as the crystal ball acts for the skrier, creating a species of self-hypnosis. Reading Nostradamus' prefaces after having made some acquaintance with the quatrains, the reader rather receives the impression that the prophet is himself groping for an explanation of what he has seen or experienced.

The publication of the *Centuries* aroused widespread interest, testimony to the fact that the author was already well known as a prophet, for until the published prophecies were fulfilled in, at least part, there was nothing to distinguish them from their many predecessors. But among the hundreds of quatrains there was one which aroused the interest of the royal family – in particular, the interest of the Queen, Catherine de' Medici. All her life she had been not so much interested in the occult – in particular the art of prophecy – as accepting it on a purely matter-of-fact basis. Among the prophets she honoured was a certain Luc Gauric, a Neapolitan who had cast her own horoscope at her birth and had recently declared that her husband, Henri II, would lose his life through a duel. The King mocked the prophecy but Catherine remembered it. The vast majority of Nostradamus' quatrains must have been as enigmatic to her as they are to posterity but one verse took her attention. It was the 35th quatrain of the 1st Century and ran:

The Young Lion shall overcome the old
In a martial field by a single duel.
In a golden cage he shall put out his eye.
Two wounds from one, then he shall die a cruel death.

Nostradamus was summoned to Paris to explain. It is highly unlikely that he could have done so with any real degree of clarity but he impressed Catherine even if her husband remained indifferent. It was from this point that his involvement with the royal family began, an involvement

L

which spread his fame yet further – and gave him protection when, inevitably, questions were raised regarding just what powers he was using to peer into the future.

In 1559, a little over eighteen months after, Henri II was killed – in a duel. The ' young lion ' who overcame him was Montgomery, the captain of his Scottish bodyguard. They were taking part in a joust to celebrate the marriage of Henri's daughter. Twice Montgomery had defeated his master and Henri, reluctant to yield to a younger man, insisted that they should ride the course again. On the third encounter both lances were shattered and, in passing, the splintered end of Montgomery's lance passed through Henri's visor and pierced his eye. For those who remembered the quatrain, it was an unnervingly accurate fulfilment, for Henri was wearing a gilded helmet – the ' golden cage ' of the quatrain and the fragmented lance not only struck him in the eye but also in the throat – ' two wounds from one '. Certainly the populace, with whom Henri had been popular, were convinced that Nostradamus must have had some hand in his death for they burnt his effigy and called upon the Church to burn him in reality.

But now he was under the direct protection of the powerful, baleful Catherine de' Medici, destined to be the effective ruler of France for the next decade and more. Already strongly disposed towards Nostradamus, the apparent working out of his prophecy convinced her that she possessed, in him, a most potent weapon for the control of the State. She ordered him to draw up the horoscopes of her seven children – those ill-fated children who were to be the very last of the house of Valois. Their fate was, in fact, already foreshadowed in the published *Centuries*. When Nostradamus had been composing the quatrains there had been no reason whatsoever to suppose that the Valois were drawing to their end. Similarly, when he told – or showed the Queen how three of her four sons would be kings of France it seemingly had not occurred to her to enquire how this could be possible.

That paradox was resolved when, over a space of thirty years, each of the three young men wore the crown in turn, and died of hereditary disease or the assassin's dagger.

The House shall die with the death of the Seven.

The fate of some were seen clearly enough: 'The first son of the widow will make an unhappy marriage and will die, without children, before his eighteenth year, leaving two Isles in discord'. That first son was Francis II, who died a few weeks short of his eighteenth birthday, leaving his widow, the unfortunate Mary, Queen of Scots, indeed to put the two islands of Britain into discord. There are vague hints of the massacre of St Bartholomew when the second son, the unbalanced Charles IX, assuaged his blood lust on the bodies of his Huguenot subjects and then, with astonishing clarity, an indication of the assassination of the third son, Henri III, by the hand of the monk Jacques Clement:

The King-King shall perish at the hand of Le Doux.

The line is an ideal example of Nostradamus' compressed highly allusive style. King-King (Roy-Roy) is an excellent description of Henri III for he was simultaneously King of Poland and of France. And Doux is one of the synonyms for *clement*. Henri was the last of the Valois. But if the story of the divining mirror can be accepted, Nostradamus had already foreshadowed the passing of the crown to the Bourbon branch, for after the three Valois brothers had made their magical circuit of the mirror, their place had been taken by their cousin, Henri of Navarre. But before even then, the young cousin had taken the prophet's attention. Henri of Navarre had been ten years old when Nostradamus drew up the horoscopes for his royal cousins. Catherine de' Medici had not been interested in the young provincial – but Nostradamus was. He asked to see the boy naked; Henri refused, less out of modesty than a wholesome fear of being beaten. Nostradamus therefore arranged with the boy's tutor to enter his bedroom at night and examine him while asleep. Whatever marks he found upon the boy's body convinced him that, in the fulness of time, it would be he who inherited the kingdom of France.

Such was the story which his disciple Chavigny included in his *Testament*. Nostradamus himself died before he could witness the accuracy of his prophecy regarding Henri of Navarre. It seems that he had foreseen his own death with his usual curious mixture of sharp precision and cloudiness:

> On returning from an embassy
> And with the King's gift safely locked away
> I shall do no more having gone to God.
> My family shall find me, dead, near my bed and bench.

' Near my bed and bench ' could perhaps be simply a lucky shot for it was reasonable to expect an old man to die in or near his bed. The bench was a device rigged up to help him move about in bed, for he had grown enormous with dropsy. But he did, in fact, die after having gone on an embassy to the King on behalf of the town. Inevitably legends grew around the manner of his death and sepulture for over the following centuries this or that quatrain has been freely interpreted as referring to the burial and what came afterwards. He was supposed to have ordered that a hidden key to the quatrain should be buried with him; alternatively, he was supposed to have predicted the removal of his corpse from one resting place to another some fifty years after his death. Certainly the coffin was opened then, and a diligent search made for the priceless document. But nothing was found.

With the known and certain date of the first publication of the *Centuries* as a vital base date and point of orientation, the reader is in a position to make his own assessment of the validity of those quatrains that are at least comprehensible. Over the past three centuries an impressive collection of Nostradamiana has come into being. Each generation tends to interpret the quatrains in terms of contemporary affairs, which

40 An eighteenth-century representation of Nostradamus'
divination by mirror for Catherine de' Medici

41 Joanna Southcott

42 The full moon directly affecting the minds of women : a seventeenth-century French engraving illustrating a traditional view of correspondence

the lack of dates and paucity of proper nouns makes it only too easy to do. In scores of the quatrains, too, there is no sense of scale so the reader is quite uncertain as to whether Nostradamus is referring to some universal calamity – or an irritation to some individual. But in the luxuriant jungle of fanciful interpretations every so often there are one or two which give pause to the most sceptical. A close knowledge of French history is a prerequisite for understanding much that referred to the two generations after Nostradamus' death – two generations in which the Valois came to an end and the Bourbons arrived in the person of Henri IV, and the quatrains are at their densest and most tantalising. But as the perspective draws away so events recognisable to any reasonably well-read European stand out above the tangle. Two of the most remarkable of the quatrains – perhaps the most remarkable of all prophetic words – refer to an event of European importance – the capture and humiliation of Louis XVI by the revolutionaries.

In June 1792 Louis and his wife Marie Antoinette took the last possible chance of escaping from France. He was dressed simply in grey, she in white, for their journey by coach. At the small town of Varennes they were recognised and an official by the name of Sauce or Saulce demanded to see their papers. They were returned to Paris where the King was further humiliated by being forced to put on the cap of liberty. The 20th quatrain of the eleventh Century traces the first part of the tragedy with eerie precision.

By night there shall come through the forest of Reines
A married couple, by a tortuous route, Herne the white
   stone
The monk in grey, within Varennes :
Elected Cap : thereafter tempest, fire, blood and cutting off.

The pinpoint of the name Varennes alone would make this a remarkable quatrain, for historically nothing else has happened in that small town save the arrest of the fleeing king.

But the last line is no less astonishing. The abbreviation Cap. is Nostradamus' usual shorthand for the ruling house : Louis was the first king to be elected – a fact worth nothing. And finally the sombre march of words that follow the arrest – tempest, fire, blood – and ending with the hideous *tranche* – to cut off – leaves very little to the imagination.

The second quatrain occurs in the same Century but is separated from the first.

> One alone shall be mitred on return
> A conflict of 500 shall pass by the tiles (le thuille)
> A traitor will be called Narbon and Saulce shall sell his oil.

The Sauce or Saulce who arrested the King was a chandler, selling oil among other commodities. The Comte of Narbonne, supposedly Louis' minister and ally, worked with the revolutionaries. And as for the rest, the dense-packed references to a crowd of 500 by the tiles – it can hardly be coincidence that shortly after Louis returned to Paris a mob of some 500 people invaded the Tuileries – the place of the tiles.

Nostradamus' cloudy gaze was concentrated, in the main, on the future of his own country. Apart from France, his major identified interest is with Britain – specifically with England. Most of these quatrains are in their usual ambiguous form with a lack of hard names and dates :

> The rejected one shall mount the throne . . .
> Her time will be exceedingly triumphant
> And she will die at seventy, in the century's third year.

This could fit, without twisting too many probabilities, with Elizabeth I, who was indeed rejected and whose reign was indeed triumphant until her death in 1603 – the century's third year. With greater precision, Nostradamus' eye lights upon Charles I – ' The senate of London shall put their king to death ' – and enemies of Cromwell have had little difficulty in seeing him as,

More resembling a butcher than a king in England
Born obscurely he shall seize power by force.

So obscurely, cloudily, the reader can follow the course of
the Rebellion and Restoration – provided he is prepared to
make a fairly generous allowance. Then, in the second
Century, two successive quatrains must bring him up short.

The blood of the just shall be required of London
Burnt by fire in thrice twenty and six
The old lady shall fall from her high place
Of the same sect many shall be destroyed.

Thrice twenty and six is sixty-six: the Fire of London
takes place in 1666. This is one of Nostradamus' very few
dates and can hardly be put down to simple coincidence,
particularly when, in a following quatrain, he refers to 'the
great plague of the maritime city which shall not cease till
the death of the just is avenged'. As far as Nostradamus was
concerned the execution of Charles I was murder and London
would have to pay for it.

Like the Delphic sybil, Nostradamus gives the impression
of a person peering into a thick cloud which at times thins,
allowing a fleeting glimpse of objects without scale or orientation. Sometimes, the cloud disappears altogether for a moment
and the seer receives the pinpoint precision of 'Varennes' or
'the London Senate'. But usually he is aware only of vague
forms and colours now coalescing, now drifting apart. After
the eighteenth century the density of the quatrains begins to
thin out as though the seer's vision grew weaker the greater
the extent of time. For the nineteenth and twentieth centuries,
however, they still remain apposite enough to allow the
erection of elaborate theories. Devoted French annotators
claimed to be able to follow the whole of the Dreyfus case
and in the Second World War Allied propagandists put out
fake – and ominous – prophecies regarding the future of
Germany based on the so-called Hister quatrains. The 24th

quatrain of the eleventh Century contains the most explicit of these supposed references to Adolf Hitler :

> Beasts maddened with hunger will move the streams,
> Hister will rule over a great part of the country,
> The great one shall be dragged into a cage of iron,
> When the child of Germany shall observe nothing.

Scattered throughout the Centuries are other references to Hister and another powerful man who might be Mussolini but who has also been confidently identified as Napoleon, among others.

Beyond the twentieth century the shadows thicken. Nevertheless, Nostradamus does not hesitate to give a term to the end of things. There will be a series of Antichrists, and then

> In the year one thousand and nine hundred ninety (and)
>   seven months
> From Heaven shall come the great king of terror.

Reasonably, this might be taken as referring either to the second coming or the end of the world in July 1999.

The *Centuries* of Nostradamus, for all their tantalising obliqueness, stand head and shoulders above all other so-called prophetic works. Even if some ninety-five per cent of the quatrains defy any attempt at clear interpretation, the remaining five per cent do retain sufficient nuggets of hard fact to render tenable the claim that Nostradamus saw something beyond the normal frontiers of time. There is no lack of claims for others. The thirteenth century poet known as Thomas the Rhymer has been frequently put forward as a kind of Scottish Nostradamus, in particular regarding his bloodcurdling prophecies for the house of Mar. Coinneach Fiossaiche, generally known as the Brahan Seer, is supposed to have discharged a similar ungrateful task for the MacKenzie clan and thrown in, for good measure, odd predictions regarding nuclear submarines, the arrival of the railway and the collapse of the Tay bridge. But, like the prophecies of Mother Shipton, the most striking of the prophecies of the Brahan Seer and Thomas the Rhymer found their way into print an embarrassingly long while after their death, attaining thereby the virtues of hindsight rather than prevision.

One of the very rare continuous prophecies, apart from the *Centuries,* are the papal prophecies of Malachy O'Morgair. Born in the eleventh century, his life was attended by the usual miracles of the holy man, including healing the mortally sick, levitation and making casual everyday prophecies. He died in November 1184 while on a visit to Bernard of Clairvaux and left among his meagre effects a series of short, enigmatic prophecies regarding the identities of the Popes until the end of the twentieth century. Most of the prophecies were cast in the form of slogans or mottoes. Thus he entitled the twentieth Pope as Signum Ostiensis: the twentieth Pope was Alexander IV, Cardinal of Ostia. The motto for Pius VI (1775-99) was *Peregrinus Apostolicus* – a curiously exact phrase for the wandering life that the unfortunate Pope was forced to lead as a result of the French Revolution. *Lumen in Caelo* was the motto that the eleventh century monk devised for the nineteenth century Pope Leo XIII – whose family coat-of-arms was a comet. Not all of the long list of pontiffs were identified with such curious precisions: many, indeed, are wholly noncommittal, as with that of the present Pope – Flower of Flowers – which seems to have no immediate bearing. But *Pastor et Nauta* for Pope John XXIII again seems remarkably apt, whether it is considered symbolically as referring to a Pope who began to alter the course of the Roman Catholic Church or merely as referring to his maritime associations as Patriarch of Venice.

Malachy lists five more Popes who shall reign after the present *Flos Forum* (Paul VI), the last Pope to ascend St Peter's chair being Peter II. Rome will then be destroyed and the Last Judgement will take place. Assuming that an average pontificate is between seven and ten years in length, Peter II will be reigning at the turn of the millennium, the end of the world taking place some time in the first decade of the twenty-first century. If the next five Popes reign for shorter periods than usual, then Malachy's prophecy for the end of the world could neatly coincide with that of Nostradamus.

Chapter 11
Apocalyptic Societies

Tarot cards and tea-leaves; flaming suns and ox liver; pyromancy and cartomancy; palmistry and skrying – varied though the means, the object remains constant and that is to peer even an hour ahead in time. For most people – perhaps the majority – the goal is essentially personal and, usually, can be summed up in two or three questions. Whom shall I marry? How much money shall I have? Will my enterprise be fortunate? How long shall I live? These are the questions which professional fortune-tellers most often meet and have long since learned to design satisfactory answers. But there are, occasionally, questions with a larger connotation, questions which are usually asked of religious or philosophic disciplines – 'Where is humanity going?' and 'When shall it get there?' The complex, inconclusive answers afforded by the established philosophies satisfy most. But there are some who need stronger meat, who prefer black and white to indeterminate greys and who argue that it is ever better to arrive than to travel. These draw aside from the formal systems and establish their own short cut to revelation, their numbers rising and falling in response to conditions in the outside world.

It was for long believed that, in the closing decades of the tenth century, Christendom was plunged into a blind panic believing that the end of the world would coincide with the opening of the new millennium. The belief was doubtless exaggerated but it was rooted in a rational premise. From the earliest days Christians had been awaiting the dissolution of all things, basing their own expectations, reasonably enough, on the unequivocal statements in the Gospels and Epistles. As the decades became centuries and the earth continued to make its way around the heavens, so the firm prophecies became symbolic. But still there was an underlying belief in the literalness of the prophecies and, as the magical year 1000 approached, so there arose certain sects who argued that this was the literal ' millennium ' promised by the Bible. How far the passionate belief of a minority of fundamentalists infected the community as a whole it is impossible now to conjecture, for nothing is quite so dead as a dead emotion. But it certainly affected those who were normally indifferent or sceptical of occultism. ' Seeing that the end of the world is now approaching' was a fairly common formula in wills executed during the second half of the tenth century.

Fundamentalists have a harder row to hoe in the twentieth century – but it would seem that three zeros in a date still has its magic potential, judging by the increasing number of organisations which, in their different ways, are preparing for the end of things. There are signs in plenty for those who seek signs: two titanic wars within a generation; the exploding of the atomic bomb; soaring populations with their concomitants of soaring pollution – all can be, and have been, used by eschatological devotees as proof that the world is gadarening down the last slopes towards the year AD 2000.

In 1942 there appeared a publication which courageously gave an exact date for the opening of the spiritual millennium and the ending of the present dispensation. *The Great Pyramid, its Christian message to all nations and its divine call to the British Empire and USA with Iceland* was its orotund title. Published by the newly-formed Institute of Pyramidology, it sought to interpret what is admittedly one of the most enduring of architectural enigmas – the Great Pyramid of Cheops. The author, Adam Rutherford, proceeded along what is now the traditional approach for the 'interpretation' of the pyramid. The argument runs, in essence, that the dimensions and internal arrangements of chambers and passages of the pyramid are too complex, too deliberate to form simply a tomb. The pyramid must therefore be a three-dimensional code which will tell a clear story to the person who possesses the key. Rutherford claimed that the key was the so-called pyramid inch, a measurement equal to 25.027 British inches. Further authentication of the pyramid's role is to be found in Isaiah 19 : ' In that age there shall be, in the centre of Egypt but at the desert edge, a monument that shall be a sign and an altar of witness . . .' The identification of this monument with Cheops' pyramid is complete when it is realised that the height of the pyramid – 5,449 pyramid inches – corresponds exactly with the Hebrew text of Isaiah if Hebrew figures are substituted for the letters in the verse. These combine to make 5,449.

The pyramid inch equals one year of earthly time and, with this key, every passage and every chamber of the pyramid can be made to yield a prophecy. Beginning at the year 2613 BC when the foundation stone was deduced to have been laid, the prophecies take the time traveller forward to the twentieth century, each crisis or major event in history being marked by some peculiarity in the construction of the pyramid. ' So much of the pyramid's chronological prophecy has now become actual history that the scale 1 inch = 1 year has been incontrovertibly proved '.

The prophecies are, unsurprisingly, accurate for events before 1942, somewhat less accurate afterwards. The architect – or interpreter – scored a definite bull's-eye with the prediction that World War II would end sometime between May and August 1945 but missed the target entirely with the confident prediction that the millennium of peace would begin in July 1953. But the individual prophecies that the pyramid has to make, though interesting, pale to nothing beside the major revelation that the British, American and Icelandic races will, between them, create a new order in the millennium that is to come. Britain's claim is substantiated by the fact that it was to Britain that Christ came, ' seeking a quiet retreat outside the Roman Empire ', before the dawning of his ministry. America's share in the great destiny arises partly from the fact that ' the USA is, of course, really a development of the British Empire ', but also by specific revelation of the pyramid. Iceland's destiny is revealed both in the pyramid and in Isaiah, where the verse, ' They shall cry aloud from the West, Wherefore glorify ye the Lord in the fires ', can naturally only apply to a volcanic island in the West.

The Institute of Pyramidology does not seem to have survived the discovery that 1953 did not, after all, spell the beginning of a divine New Order. Outright refutation of a treasured theory does not, however, necessarily destroy the faith of devotees : if this were the case, the followers of Joanna Southcott would have disbanded themselves in 1927. It was in that year that her famous Box was opened and found to contain only a few odds and ends of no conceivable value or interest to anyone. The Panacea Society, which inherited Joanna Southcott's burden, merely declared that the box which had been opened was not her box and continued their work of propagation.

Joanna Southcott was born in Devonshire about 1750 and worked as a domestic servant for the greater part of her life. In her early forties she became convinced that she had supernatural gifts and began to dictate a spate of rhyming prophecies. The English had, perhaps, grown somewhat indifferent to prophets and it was not until she announced that, in her sixties, she would be delivered of the child Shiloh on 19 October 1814 as prophesied in Revelation that she achieved national fame. In 1814 in her 64th year she did indeed appear to be pregnant and her followers attended her day and night, waiting for the miraculous birth. But nothing happened on the expected day and she died – of dropsy – on the 29th.

Superficially, there seems nothing to distinguish Joanna Southcott from a larger number of eccentric elderly ladies: even the phantom pregnancy is a common enough psychosomatic effect. But in 1898 the magisterial *Encyclopedia Britannica* noted, with an air of surprise: 'Her followers are said to have numbered over 100,000 and so late as 1860 they were not extinct.' But neither were they extinct a century later.

The key to the success of the Southcottians lay in the air of mystery which surrounded her famous box. Among the masses of revelations which she dictated were some which she was divinely instructed not to publish but was to seal up in an 'Ark or Box' which was to be opened, in the presence of twenty-four bishops, only in a time of national danger. In 1927 Harry Price, the psychic investigator, opened what was claimed to be the nailed and sealed box in the presence of a large crowd – but with only one bishop in attendance, a fact which apparently had an adverse effect upon its revelatory contents. At regular intervals since then the Panacea Society has petitioned the Archbishop of Canterbury to empanel the twenty-four bishops necessary. As regularly, successive archbishops have refused to do so, disagreeing with the Society that 'Manifestly, as the Christian religion has been built upon prophecy, it *must* be the bounden duty of the Heads of the Church to look into everything purporting to be a Divine Revelation laid up for this country'.

Despite the fact that the world is deprived of the sealed teachings, Joanna Southcott's followers have been able to evolve a complex and detailed picture of the true Revelation. There are not one, but three classes of 'Human' beings. The first are Anthropoids, descendants of pre-Adamic races who have no souls 'and are now about to be annihilated. They are manifesting today as Bolshevists and Communists and are about to destroy each other in a visible and very active hell – Russia and all countries which are falling under Red influence.' The second class are the Incorruptibles – what most people would call normal human beings whose bodies die and whose souls go to heaven. The third and most important class are the Immortals, those living on earth now who will never know death, thanks to the Society's mission of healing. They will come into their own in the first few seconds of the twenty-first century. The Adamic Age – consisting of a Divine Week of six days of a thousand years each – comes to an end in AD 2000; thereafter a literal, physical Kingdom of God will be established on Earth.

In 1614 a German scholar by name of Johann Valentin Andreae launched, with German thoroughness, a heavy practical joke. The scholars of Europe were invited – urged – to join a secret society, supposedly founded by a certain Christian Rosenkreuz two centuries earlier. Rosenkreuz bore such obvious affinities to Munchausen and Sir John Mandeville that it is surprising that any reasonably well-read person was taken in. He had travelled – inevitably – in the East and acquired a great store of occult knowledge which Europeans were now invited to test for themselves.

Andreae's joke misfired: it was, in fact, too good. Within a year or so of the publication of his treatise a large controversial literature had sprung up either condemning the pretensions of the Rosicrucians – as they were known – or warmly supporting their claim to have direct access to occult truths. Andreae was forgotten in the tumult that followed. In England, the scholarly Robert Fludd seized on the purely notional Order as a means of giving a shape and form to his weird theory that man was an exact, if miniature, replica of the universe. The great Kepler himself condescended to show up the gaping holes in Fludd's cosmos but, nevertheless, by the end of the seventeenth century Rosicrucianism was established as a fact of life and over the next two centuries its appeal would rise and fall in response to the intellectual climate of the day.

The twentieth-century resurrection of the Ancient and Mystical Order Rosae Crucis seems to have owed its initial impulse to Max Heindel in America, shortly after he had parted with the Theosophists: both draw upon exotic, Eastern concepts to colour what is an essentially amorphous structure; both are eclectic; both – naturally – lay claim to possession of the ultimate and unique truth regarding human destiny. But Rosicrucianism presents a crisper, more 'modern' face to the world. Its sprawling headquarters in San Jose, California, are reminiscent of the Mormon headquarters in Utah. Much play is made of the exotic tradition of ancient Egyptian wisdom, even down to influencing the architecture. At times, the visitor might be forgiven for wondering if he had strayed into a film set for *Caesar and Cleopatra* so powerful is this influence. Nevertheless, administratively, the order is a model of 'business efficiency' – not least through the very modern technique of correspondence courses through which the neophyte can hope to progress to the highest levels of 'cosmic consciousness'. Confidence is, perhaps, the most obvious attribute of Rosicrucianism. The dubious origins in seventeenth century Germany have long since been forgotten: the Rosicrucian now looks to ancient Egypt as the cradle of his order and there is no hesitation in identifying ancient Egyptians who nurtured the cult. But neither is there any hesitation in identifying as a Rosicrucian all the more wholesome great during the past three millennia from Dante to Harriet Beecher Stowe. The catalogue of books published by the order – most of them by the same author – similarly assert with confidence what others suggest with diffidence. The source for *The Mystical Life of Jesus Christ* corrects, and predates, the Dead Sea Scrolls, 'indicating a secret source of information known only to the author'. The discovery of a unique and secret source of information relating to the life of Christ argues research ability of an astonishingly high order, an argument substantiated by the claim that another book was 'translated by special permission of the Grand Lama and Disciples of the Sacred College in the Grand Temple of Tibet'. This vital document was presumably overlooked by Madame Blavatsky and her mahatmas alike. The Great

M

Pyramid is again made to prophesy – although with different results to those of the Institute of Pyramidology, reincarnation authoritatively established, the sceptic finally refuted. Altogether, Johann Valentin Andreae has good reason to congratulate himself on the durable qualities of his practical joke.

Apocalyptic, revelationary societies tend to change their form rather than their substance. Each new one rings the changes on a strictly limited number of concepts. Wisdom is, invariably, located only in the East – preferably in Tibet, ancient Egypt or India. China, with its civilisation of vast antiquity, curiously enough contributes little. The old is, by definition, more accurate, more wise than the new : knowledge is to be found in Atlantis, not Atlantic City, and books printed in black letter are, *ipso facto*, more likely to be keys to the occult than books employing Times Roman. But, almost imperceptibly, the twentieth century is making its mark upon the traditional by placing a technological imprint upon part, at least, of the revelations. A Rosicrucian newsletter nods familiarly towards the RNA and DNA of the living cell; *The Occult Gazette* announces ' Uranian Glory as Divine Molecular Unity ' and goes on to talk of the ' Atomic polarised divinity of the soul '.

Undoubtedly the most outstanding among the tiny but growing class of the technological/occult is the Aetherius Society with its successful fusion of the traditional and the modern. The initial driving power came from an Indian Swami but the society continues to operate through the medium of Flying Saucers.

In May 1954 the Reverend Doctor George King was warned by telepathy that he was to become the first voice of an Interplanetary Parliament – the ' Primary Terrestrial Mental Channel '. A few days later he was visited, in his London apartment, by a person who seemed, from outward appearances, to be an ordinary human being, or Earth man. His visitor was an Indian Swami who had projected himself astrally, but tangibly, from India in order to prepare George

King for his mission. Not long afterwards he took off on his first interplanetary visit. His goal was Venus, but it proved to be not possible to land because the Venusians had drawn a protective magnetic girdle about their planet. He was, however, welcomed, as he was under the protection of the Master Aetherius and later took part in a titanic battle between Venus and the sinister planet Mars, when he gave a good account of himself in telepathic warfare.

In his various books, Dr King gives considerable technical information both about the Venusian Flying Saucers, with their ability to travel faster than light, and the military and social activities of the non-terrestrial beings. But the main interest is centred upon the establishment of a contact-system on Earth. After his return from Venus, Dr King met the Master Jesus on the top of Holdstone Down in Devonshire – the first hill or mountain to be charged as a cosmic battery. Nine other mountains were charged in Britain before Dr King crossed the Atlantic to charge four more mountains in the USA and to establish the American section of the society in Los Angeles. Over the next three years he circumnavigated the globe, charging yet more mountains with cosmic energy in Australasia and Europe.

The object of the society is to maintain, via Dr King, telepathic contact with non-terrestrial beings of advanced intelligence. These beings include the Master Aetherius, of Venus; the entity calling itself Mars Sector 6; the Master Jesus – commonly but erroneously believed to have been crucified about the year AD 33 and someone or something calling itself Jupiter 92. Ultimately, through these ' adepts ', or teachers, mankind will advance into a state of cosmic consciousness, interplanetary existence and the attainment of his true spiritual self. But the contact with these intelligences also has immediate practical value. In January and February 1962 occurred that configuration of the planets which warned of the impending destruction of the Earth. Jupiter, however, put out immense pulses of spiritual energy which were channelled through the terrestrial members of the Aetherius Society.

While millions slept in blissful, but dangerous ignorance, the Aetherius Society Directors and members tuned in to be used as channels for the great Transmuting Energies. Jupiter saved the Earth and used the Aetherius Society to do so.

It would seem that the full circle has been made, for the Babylonian seers, on their high artificial hills, looked upon their task as essentially the same.

Short Bibliography

Balleine, G. R. *Past finding out: the tragic story of Joanna Southcott and her successors* 1956

Collin, Rodney *The theory of celestial influence* 1955

Cooke, Christopher *Curiosities of occult literature* 1863

Cumont, Franz *Astrology and religion among the Greeks and Romans* 1923

de Wohl, Louis *The stars of War and Peace* 1952

Dollinger, J. J. *Prophecies and the prophetic spirit* (trans. Alfred Plummer) 1873

Dunne, J. W. *An experiment with time* 1927

Eisler, Robert *The royal art of astrology* 1946

Flammarion, C. *History of the Heavens* (trans. J. F. Blake)

Fox, R. J. *The finding of Shiloh or the mystery of God 'finished'* n.d.

Gauquelin, M. *L'influence des Astres* 1955

Gleadow, R. *The origin of the Zodiac* 1968

Howe, Ellic *Urania's children: the strange world of the astrologers* 1967

Jung, C. G. *The integration of the personality* (trans. S. M. Dell) 1946

Laver, James *Nostradamus: or the future foretold* 1952

Lewis, H. Spence *Rosicrucian questions and answers with complete History of the Rosicrucian Order* 1954

Ptolemy, C. *Tetrabiblos* (trans. J. M. Ashmond) 1822

Rhine, J. B. *New frontiers of the mind* 1938

Sachs, A., ' Babylonian horoscopes' in *Journal of Cuneiform Studies* Vol. VI

Southcott, Joanna *Book of Wonders* 1813-14

Thompson, R. C. (ed.) *The reports of the magicians and astrologers of Nineveh and Babylon* 1900

Thorndike, Lynn *A history of magic and experimental science*

Velikovsky, I. *Worlds in collision*

Wedel, T.O. 'The medieval attitude towards astrology' in *Yale Studies in English* LX 1920

Index